GREAT RUNNING BACKS

GREAT RUNNING BACKS

FOOTBALL'S FEARLESS FOOT SOLDIERS

STEVE HUBBARD

MetroBooks

MetroBooks

An Imprint of Friedman/Fairfax Publishers

Library of Congress Cataloging-in-Publication Data

Hubbard, Steve (Steve A)
    Running backs : football's fearless foot soldiers / Steve Hubbard.
        p.   cm.
    Includes bibliographical references and index.
    ISBN 1-56799-297-8 (hc)
        1. Running backs (Football)--United States--Bibliography. I. Title
GV939.A1H83 1996
796.332'092'2--dc20
[B]   95-51985
                                                              CIP

Editor: Stephen Slaybaugh
Art Director: Jeff Batzli
Design: Stan Stansky
Photography Editor: Wendy Missan

Color separations by HBM Print Ltd.
Printed in China by Leefung Asco Printers Ltd.

For bulk purchases and special sales, please contact:
Friedman/Fairfax Publishers
Attention: Sales Department
15 West 26th Street
New York, NY 10010
212/685-6610 FAX 212/685-1307

Visit the Friedman/Fairfax Website:
http://www.webcom.com/friedman/

DEDICATION

To my parents, who gave me my work ethic; and to my wife, who gave me happiness.

ACKNOWLEDGMENTS

This book would be a lesser one without the insights and anecdotes of NFL players, ex-players, coaches, and front-office men—particularly Andy Russell, Ray Mansfield, Gale Sayers, Bucko Kilroy, George Young, Ted Marchibroda, and Bill Tobin. I am indebted to Steve Sabol of NFL Films, Don Smith of the Pro Football Hall of Fame, and the NFL public relations people, especially Bryan Harlan of the Bears and Craig Kelley of the Colts. Thanks to writers Greg Garber, Peter King, Vic Carucci, Ed Werder, and Bryan Burwell, among others, who shared their wisdom and wealth of information. And finally, a special thanks to my editors: Nathaniel Marunas, for showing faith that I could write this book, and Stephen Slaybaugh, for making it a reality.

CONTENTS

INTRODUCTION

The night before my call, Ray Mansfield had gone to a cigar dinner, the kind where grown men sit around smoking fat stogies, sipping wine, and telling tall tales.

Everyone from tattooed motorcyclists in black leather to proper surgeons in Armani suits gathered round as the Ol' Ranger recounted his days as a stout two-way lineman for the Philadelphia Eagles and the Pittsburgh Steelers. He had played with Mean Joe and Jack Splat, Franco and Webby, and Bradshaw and Swann. He had played against O.J. and Sweetness, Butkus and Brown, and Staubach and Stabler, but in between puffs on his big, Churchill-size La Gloria Cubana, the story he told was about a kick return.

It happened nearly thirty years ago and the return was made by the Kansas Comet, Gale Sayers.

"I was telling about when we opened the 1967 season," Mansfield said. "We kicked off to the Bears, and Gale Sayers took the ball 3 yards deep in the end zone and ran about 225 yards for a touchdown. He ran by each guy on the kickoff team about three times. He caught it left of the goal post and went right, should have been tackled at about the 10, came almost straight across the 20 yard line, then cut back again when he got to the other sideline and ended up running up the right sideline. It was incredible. People got up and had two shots at him. There was nothing open; he was just making it on his own. He was elusive as I've ever seen."

This is what the great runners do: they leave grown men reminiscing about great moves and great games even three decades later. They captivate little boys, sending them rushing to the sporting-goods store to buy their jerseys, and to the playground to try to duplicate their idol's dazzling moves.

After bulling for 112 yards in Super Bowl VII to cap the NFL's only perfect season, bruiser Larry Csonka ran for a then-record 145 yards and 2 scores the following year to help the Dolphins beat the Vikings and earn himself Super Bowl VIII MVP honors.

ABOVE: **Natrone Means, who led the Chargers to the Super Bowl in his first season as a starter, is a Brahma bull back of the nineties.**

OPPOSITE: **Tony Dorsett, who led the Cowboys to a Super Bowl victory as a rookie, was a bumblebee back of the seventies and eighties.**

We can all identify with the runners, because in some way, whether it was playing dodgeball, avoiding the tag in baseball or flag football, or mimicking Elgin Baylor, Dr. J, or Michael Jordan to shake free in basketball, we have all tried to do what they do. But the great ones take the sport's most distinctly instinctive skill to a higher level, performing with such style and grace, such strength and speed, that we can only marvel. They turn little boys' dreams into reality.

The great ones don't leave us with only records and rotisserie numbers; they leave us with indelible memories. They leave their footprints not just in the mud, grass, or AstroTurf, but in the mind's eye.

Some backs, like Jim Thorpe in the teens, Red Grange in the twenties, Steve Van Buren in the forties, Hugh McElhenny in the fifties, Gale Sayers in the sixties, O.J. Simpson in the seventies, Tony Dorsett in the eighties, and Barry Sanders in the nineties, evade tacklers as if they had radar detectors in their eyes and lightning in their feet.

Others, like Bronko Nagurski in the thirties, Marion Motley in the forties, Jim Brown in the fifties and sixties, Larry Csonka in the seventies, Earl Campbell in the eighties, and Jerome Bettis and Natrone Means in the nineties, run over people like a twenty-team mule train.

Jim Brown, here avoiding a straight arm from the Giants' Spider Lockhart, was a perfect combination of size, speed, and power. He led the league in rushing eight of his nine seasons, made the Pro Bowl each year, and never missed a game.

"They say sports are supposed to fill you with wonder," said Steve Sabol, who, as son of the founder of NFL Films and now its president, has watched thousands of highlight hours. "Well, Jim Brown was the first athlete who ever did that for me. Gale Sayers was the same way. He was the one guy who if you took your eyes off him, you could miss what I like to call heirloom plays. They're plays that are passed down from generation to generation, that fathers tell their sons about. 'Yeah, you should have seen the day Gale Sayers scored 6 touchdowns in the mud.' Or, 'You should have seen the day Gale Sayers faked Lenny Lyles right out of his shoes.'"

Oh, the stories we could tell...

ABOUT JIM BROWN...

Former Steeler Andy Russell: "He was the best I ever played against. My rookie year, in Cleveland, I must have had 10 open shots at him, absolutely open shots because he was getting through our line. I probably missed him half the time. He'd make you miss one time and the next time you'd be worried about that and he'd run right over you. I was really humiliated, having missed that many tackles. That's not exactly quality linebacking. But when we watched films, the coach said, 'If we didn't have this rookie, we wouldn't have made any tackles.' That was our perspective on Jim Brown."

Sabol: "The Mount Everest of running backs. Where you have to start with Jim Brown is that although many are compared to Jim Brown, I've never heard Jim Brown compared to anyone else. Of all the backs in NFL history who carried more than 1,000 times, only Brown averaged more than 5 yards. He averaged 104 yards a game. He led the league in rushing his first year, and his last year he was MVP. He played nine seasons and was never diminished. You never remember him like Franco [Harris] or O.J. [Simpson]or a lot of the others, sort of playing out the string. He quit at his best. Critics said, 'All Brown can do is run,' to which Paul Brown replied, 'All Picasso can do is paint.'"

ABOUT GALE SAYERS...

Russell: "I was a junior at Missouri and someone said, 'We ought to go watch the freshmen play.' That wasn't something you normally do; we already got more than our fill of football. But he told me, 'Missouri's got a real good running back and so does Kansas.' We had Johnny Roland, who became an All-American running back and All-American safety and NFL Rookie of the Year. And Kansas had some guy who was supposed to be pretty good, too. I remember thinking, 'Good running backs are a dime a dozen.' Well, Missouri kicks off and Gale Sayers takes it 98 yards. Kansas kicks off and Roland takes it 91. The final was 48–41—and Sayers scored 7 touchdowns and Roland scored 6. It was the damnedest thing you ever saw."

Sabol: "The most exciting running back of all time was Gale Sayers. Sayers was to football what Dr. J was to basketball. Sayers had the capacity to create a moment of pure wonder. You see it and say, 'How did he do that?' Sayers had an instinctive feel for open space. It was like he had eyes all around his head. You look at his moves, and each one was an original. There were things I've never seen before and I've never seen again. He was an authentic original."

ABOUT O.J. SIMPSON...

Russell: "I remember a Pro Bowl where O.J. did a couple of things in practice that were just incredible. There was a quick pitch to him, and the defensive end penetrated upfield for what normally would have been a loss of 4 or 5 yards. All of a sudden, O.J. made a move, and the defensive end couldn't have gotten him if it were just tag football. He was just clutching air. Everybody said, 'Did you see that? Was that as amazing to you as it was to me?'

"If you based it on Steelers history, O.J. was the best. We keyed on him. We changed our defense to be more cautious. We were the leading defensive team. We had eight guys in the Pro Bowl. We didn't think anybody could run the ball on us—and he had

227 yards. I remember a coach telling us, 'Your problem is you've overpursued. Wait for him to come back to you.' Boy, was that a strategy! Pine Edwards let him bounce outside and he went 88 yards. We were in shock."

Mansfield: "That was the season [1975] we could have been perfect. They had him trapped in the backfield in like a U pocket. He had to back up 2 or 3 yards to get out of pocket, came around end and went almost 90 yards. Mike Wagner wasn't the fastest guy, but he had such an angle on him, had 10 yards on him, and O.J. just ran away from everybody!"

ABOUT THE GREATEST EVER...

Bucko Kilroy, an NFL player, coach, or personnel man since 1943, ranks Brown, Simpson, and Van Buren at the top. He picks Sayers next, then lumps Walter Payton with Dorsett, Sanders, Emmitt Smith, and Marshall Faulk.

O.J. Simpson, shown here knifing through the Denver Broncos, will be remembered by today's generation for the murder trial of the century, but football experts will remember him alongside Jim Brown, Walter Payton, and Gale Sayers as one of the greatest runners ever.

Hall of Famers Ray Nitschke, Frank Gifford, Joe Schmidt, Willie Brown, and Sam Huff all say Brown was the best. Pat Summerall, an NFL player or announcer since 1958, also says Brown. Floyd Peters and Ted Marchibroda, NFL players and coaches since the fifties, list Brown first, followed by Simpson and Sayers.

Sabol lists Brown, Simpson, Sayers, and McElhenny as the top runners, but calls Payton "the greatest running back of all time" because he also excelled at receiving, blocking, and even passing, punting, and returning. Colts boss Bill Tobin, the former Bears personnel guru, agrees. So did Payton contemporary Darryl Grant.

"Walter Payton is the all-time greatest," the Redskins defensive tackle proclaimed. "Remember the word all-time! All-time means that he's the greatest since they started keeping records. Maybe there was some other guy, who is now unknown to man, who carried a stone for more yards. Or maybe those guys who carried messages from city to city covered more yardage. You know, the guys in Greece. But as far as we know, Payton's the greatest."

Sayers called Brown "the greatest," but said you can't compare players from different eras. Giants general manager George Young agreed, saying that you can't rank them, you can only determine which backs dominated their eras. "That's the key. I said when Jim Brown retired, 'It won't be his record; it's the fact he dominated for nine years.' Shoot, that was the greatness of Jim Brown. Eventually, somebody will break a record.

"I always use Johnny Weismuller as an example. At one time he held fifty swimming records. Fifty! They're all broken now, but he dominated his period. It's the same with the guy who won six gold medals in the Olympics [Mark Spitz]. He dominated his era."

This is a book about dominators. About thrillers.

Sit back. Read. Remember. Relive. Enjoy.

Let the stories and arguments begin. Isn't that what fine wine and fat cigars are for?

Walter Payton, shown diving over a pile of linemen for a few of his 177 yards against the Eagles, owns the NFL records for rushing and combined yards.

CHAPTER ONE

THE ARTISTS

Gale Sayers improvised better than Robin Williams and made more people swing and miss than Nolan Ryan. He was the man with a million moves and was maybe the most elusive runner ever. He left defenders grasping at air, gasping in awe, and asking, "How'd he do that?"

And you know what? Sayers probably wondered the same thing.

Like most sensational backs, he didn't work on his moves, and he sure couldn't explain them. His shiftiness was a gift, an instinct, not the product of some master plan or exhaustive practice.

"I had great peripheral vision," said Sayers, the youngest man ever inducted into the Hall of Fame. "I could see everybody on the field, and so I knew where to run, where to cut. I know times I'd watch films later and there'd be a fellow from my blind side and no way I could see him, but I could feel him. You can't do anything to develop that. You can't really do any exercises. It's a God-given talent, like quickness, like the ability to cut.

"To be honest, I never worked on anything concerning running. The only thing I did was get myself in shape and learn my plays. As far as 'I'm going to run down the field and fake left and go right,' or 'I'm going to spin or stiff-arm or change the ball to the right hand or left hand,' hey, that was natural. Even in midget football, I scored something like 50 touchdowns in 7 games. Hell, I had it then.

"I always felt one on one, I could beat anybody 100 percent of the time. Two on one, I could beat them 75

percent of the time. One on one, you've got no chance. No chance! Nobody could tackle me one on one."

Coax the great backs long enough, and eventually they'll reveal a trick or two. This is Sayers' secret:

"I practiced for the unexpected," the great Bear said. "The guard is pulling; what if he falls down? Or what if the tackle is playing against Deacon Jones and he has no chance of beating him? I looked for the unexpected, and I think that's why you saw so many cutbacks, because many times, our people got beaten at the line of scrimmage. And so many times, that four or five or seven hole is closed up. Now, where do I go from there? I'm looking all over the field for that hole to cut back into.

OPPOSITE: **Gale Sayers leaps headfirst over the San Francisco 49ers defensive line for one of his record-tying 6 touchdowns on December 12, 1965.**

ABOVE: **Barry Sanders breaks free of the Vikings for a 64-yard TD en route to 110 yards and 2 scores on December 17, 1994. He and Sayers are probably the two most elusive runners ever.**

"Some people, you run a play and say it's to the four hole, come hell or high water, they're going to the four hole. They could have fifteen men there and they're going to the four hole. Hey, if there's traffic there, I'm not gonna go to the four hole. I may go to the six hole. I may go back to the one hole. Some players can't react that fast. They may not have the great peripheral vision I had. But if it's closed up, you have to do something else. You can't just run in there. This is what I was looking for. I looked for the unexpected. And many times it happened."

You rarely see today's running backs go from sideline to sideline the way Gale Sayers and Hugh McElhenny and so many other waterbugs did years ago.

Baltimore Colts coach Ted Marchibroda and ex-linebacker Andy Russell said that today's defenses are too fast and too well schooled in pursuit angles to allow it. But Sayers said that he could still do it today, that Barry Sanders does it, and that it's a combination of instincts and peripheral vision, not of speed, which is something many teams put too much emphasis on when scouting for running backs.

O.J. Simpson had that world-class speed, but he also had uncommon moves, size, and strength. He was a physical runner who said he got better the more he got the ball because he eventually stopped thinking about the game plan and scouting reports and started reacting instinctively.

O.J. Simpson became the first back to top 2,000 yards, running for 2,003 yards and a dozen scores in 1973, and followed that up with 1,817 yards and 16 TDs in 1975.

The bigger the game, the better Franco Harris played. He scored 2 touchdowns in the AFC title game and earned a then-record 158 yards to win Most Valuable Player honors as the Steelers won the first of their four Super Bowls in a six-year span, 16–6 over the Minnesota Vikings in Super Bowl IX. He finished with 354 yards and 4 TDs in four Super Bowls and 1,556 yards and 16 TDs in 19 postseason games.

"I would rather juke and try to make guys miss, but I carried the ball so much, I was a pretty physical player also," he told NFL Films. "Normally what you would do, you'd pick out a defensive back, especially an undersized DB, and you'd bowl him over a few times. That'd make it easier to juke him later on. And I wore very few pads because I wanted to feel people touching me so I could react to it."

Freeman McNeil, a top-twenty back with more than 8,000 yards rushing, said he was so sure he'd make the first guy miss that he mentally eliminated him and automatically looked downfield, figuring out how to elude the next wave.

Steve Sabol has found that trait common among the move men. "Marcus Allen has it. Hugh McElhenny.

Tony Dorsett. They have what I describe as layered vision. They can see several moves ahead, like experienced chess players, see the field like a tapestry, and can read a texture on the fly. Sayers was the greatest of all like that."

"When I get the ball," Dorsett told NFL Films, "my eyes light up like silver dollars. I'm just looking at everything. I see everything. Running the football is instinctive. It's all creative, all impromptu. Things are happening very, very quickly, and my vision helped me survive in the NFL.

"I don't want to be a bulldog runner. I'm a runner that you, your grandmother, or someone else will enjoy watching because I'm so exciting. It can happen at any time."

Franco Harris was big enough to be a bulldog runner, but the Pittsburgh Steelers fullback often ran like a tailback. "He faked me out so badly, one time I got a 15-yard penalty for grabbing my own face mask," Dallas' D.D. Lewis said. But where Dorsett would wait just a nanosecond and then accelerate through the hole, Harris would stop, wait for a hole to open, and if it didn't, he'd cut back across the field.

"The hunt and peck," Sabol said. "Franco had great timing and intelligence. He had good knee action. In many ways, he ran like O.J. The difference between a great back and a good back is they can see the seam and know when to cut against the grain. Marcus Allen does it. Eric Dickerson could do it. Franco could do it."

And then there was Jim Brown, who could do anything he wanted. He could run over a defender one time and make him miss the next, but he would always have him trembling because the defender never knew what to expect. Brown could pirouette or pulverize. Sabol has spent a lot of time studying films of this great back to find his secret.

"[Brown] led the league in rushing every year except one, and that was in 1962, when I think he played most of that year with a broken wrist," Sabol said. "That's important, because he didn't use a stiff-arm the way Marcus Allen does, but he used his arm like a crowbar. He'd keep his arm by his knees, and when a tackler hit him, he'd just sort of pry the guy off with his arms.

"He had this odd sliding stride, with his feet close to the ground. When he got hit, he'd take the shock with both feet on the ground and he never got hurt. That would be the opposite of a Roger Craig or a Lenny Moore, with their high knee action, where one leg would get clipped and they'd fall down. Brown had a way of absorbing a tackle. Certain backs—like Walter Payton and Jim Taylor and Earl Campbell—would coil when a tackler would explode into them. But Brown was exactly the opposite. He'd let his body relax, and when the tackler felt that, he thought Brown was going down and then Brown would turn on that amazing leg drive and break the tackle.

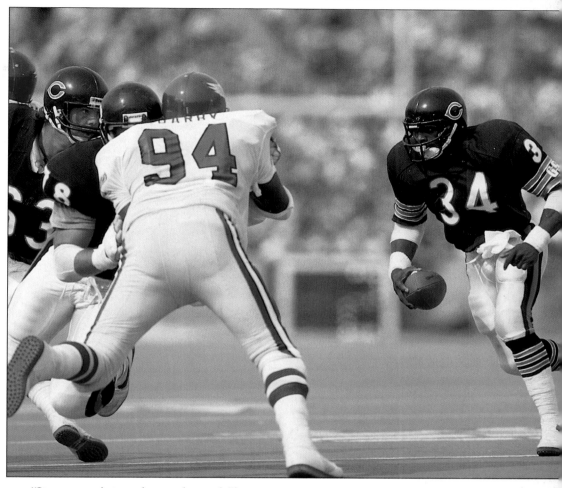

"It was an interesting style, and I've never seen anybody else use that. I've looked at film for a long time trying to figure out how he could break as many tackles as he did. He said that he didn't do it consciously in the beginning, but later he realized he would take the impact of the blow and absorb it and then explode through the tackle."

Whereas Brown rarely put his head down, Payton often did. When he could not avoid contact, Payton would explode into the defender, driving with his legs, head, and shoulder, just as his college coach had told him to: "Never die easy. Die hard." He was only five feet eleven inches and 202 pounds, but as ex-teammate Mike Adamle once said, "There are a number of defensive backs in the league with fewer neck vertebrae," referring to Payton's stiff-arm.

OPPOSITE: Jim Brown, shown here diving for a touchdown against the Baltimore Colts, set scoring records that endured for more than thirty years.

ABOVE: Walter Payton, pound for pound perhaps the toughest back in NFL history, punished would-be tacklers more than they hurt him. "Whenever an opposing defensive player is getting ready to tackle you, let him know he is being hit," not-so Sweetness said. "That's why just before I'd get tackled, I'd explode into the defensive man and sometimes I'd break away or sometimes drive for extra yardage."

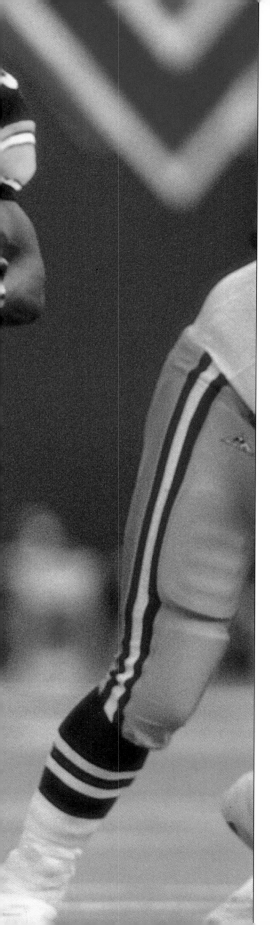

Although Payton often looked like a bull charging a matador's cape, he described his style as the flight of the bumblebee. He ran with his hamstring, hip flexor, and buttocks muscles more than with his knees. Most backs bend their knees 90 degrees from a straight line; Payton ran in a stiff-legged scissors stride, swinging his hips and bending his knees only about 30 degrees. He was up on his toes, never planting his foot long enough for anyone to take out his knees. This was not instinct, but the product of endless hours of running up hills about 60 degrees steep. He wrapped so much tape around the heels of his training shoes that they resembled high heels; his heels couldn't hit the ground if they wanted to. That's why, even though he needed arthroscopic surgery on both knees, he ran for 1,400 yards in 1983.

At age five, Emmitt Smith started sneaking off against his mother's wishes to play tackle football with his older cousins. He quickly learned that it was better to make the big guys miss. He'd watch runners on television, especially his hero O.J., then go outside "shadow running," mimicking the moves, shouting, "The Juice is on the loose!"

But now it's all instinct. For instance, in Super Bowl XXVIII, on 3 of the 6 power-right runs that produced the go-ahead score, Pro Bowl guard Nate Newton missed the key block and Smith had to abandon the original play.

"I went anywhere I wanted," Smith told the *Dallas Morning News*. "I'm going to run the play I'm supposed to run. But after I take that football in my hands, there is no telling where the hell I'm going."

The same can be said of Barry Sanders. If Sayers isn't the most electrifying runner ever, Sanders probably is. The many tackles he's broken are the product of hard work; he has gained 28 pounds since high school, most of it in those rock-hard thighs, running hills and stadium steps, and squatting as much as 600 pounds. But many of those hummingbird moves were there the instant he started playing tag and keepaway as a kid.

"Do I practice any of that stuff? No, are you kidding me?" the pride of the Lions asked the *Detroit News*. "How do you practice that stuff? You can't. It may be a lot of just God-given talent. I mean, I have been playing ball for a long time. And I can remember playing tackle football in the sandlots when I was real young, and I was playing with all the older guys and even then I was making folks miss me."

So there you have it. You can borrow a few moves, but you can't buy the great ones. You can only be given them. Good luck getting them. And to those who must tackle the gifted ones, good luck to you too.

Emmitt Smith, a strong, instinctive, and durable runner, is on pace to break Walter Payton's all-time rushing record.

CHAPTER TWO

THE BRUISERS

Just the sound of the names brings back the bruises. Bronislau Nagurski. "When you hit him," said Red Grange, "it was like getting an electric shock. If you hit him above the ankles, you were likely to get yourself killed."

Ernie Nevers. Nevers was so tough he played with a broken leg and scored 40 points in a single game, the longest-standing record in NFL history. "The final score: Bears 6, Nevers 40," moaned Bears owner George Halas.

Larry Csonka. "When he goes on safari, the lions roll up their windows," then–Detroit coach Monte Clark said of the fullback.

Earl Campbell. "All you can do," said Dallas safety Cliff Harris, "is close your eyes and hope he doesn't break your helmet."

Jim Brown. "Every time I tackle Jim Brown," defensive back Don Burroughs said, "I hear a dice game going on inside my mouth."

Darryl Johnston. Every time the Cowboys cult hero gets the ball, 65,000 Texans scream "Moooose!" The Cowboys played an exhibition game in Mexico City, and 100,000 Mexicans cried out "Moooose!"

John Henry Johnson. Johnson is so nasty that he broke Les Richter's jaw when the Ram tried to tackle him. Then, when Richter's teammates tried to retaliate, John Henry picked up a yard marker and slashed the air as if he were a mad swordsman.

Ah, so many bruising fullbacks...

Nagurski was a great runner, blocker, and tackler, and even was a professional wrestler. Nevers could run,

kick, pass, and score—he completed 17 passes in a row and scored 26 points in the same game—and played an incredible 1,711 of 1,740 possible minutes during the Duluth Eskimos' 1926 barnstorming tour. The great Pop Warner also coached Jim Thorpe but called Nevers "the greatest player I ever coached." Nevers also played major league baseball and professional basketball. He was inducted into the Pro Football Hall of Fame despite playing just five seasons.

Both Marion Motley and Joe Perry began their careers in the NFL's rival All-America Football

OPPOSITE: Nagurski finishes off a 15-yard run by diving across the goal line, scoring the first touchdown of the game in which his Washington Huskies beat Santa Clara.

LEFT: Bronislau "Bronko" Nagurski was the ultimate tough guy back in the days when the helmets were leather and the quarterbacks didn't wear skirts. Legend has it he knocked over a mounted policeman and his horse one time, put a crack in Wrigley Field's brick wall another time, and sheared the fender off a Ford on yet another occasion. "I don't know if I cracked the wall," he said years later. "I have a feeling it was cracked before. But I did hit it pretty hard."

Conference. Motley was a 238-pound moose with the speed of a deer. Perry was a 200-pound sprinter who also led both leagues in rushing and was so quick off the snap that he was nicknamed "the Jet." The first player ever to record back-to-back 1,000-yard seasons, Perry had run for more yards than anyone save Jim Brown when he retired in 1963.

When John Henry Johnson quit in 1966, only Brown, Perry, and Jim Taylor had run for more yards—and running wasn't even what John Henry did best. A great athlete, Johnson led the fabled Bob Mathias in the 1952 Olympic decathlon trials until a sprained ankle forced him out. He could run, pass, catch passes, return punts and kickoffs, and play defensive back. He was named Canadian Football League MVP as a rookie in 1953, then joined Perry, Hugh McElhenny, and Y.A. Tittle to give the 49ers a quartet of future Hall of Famers in "The Million-Dollar Backfield."

Perry and Johnson finished first and second, respectively, in NFL rushing that year. Johnson had been giving Perry running room with blocks that line coach Phil Bengtson called the best he'd ever seen. "I played

Earl Campbell led the AFC in rushing his first four years and earned the admiration of his quarterback, Dan Pastorini. "I've seen him take some hellacious hits and I've seen him deliver some hellacious hits," Pastorini said. "He's built low to the ground, and his leg strength is awesome. His legs are as big as my waist."

against Bronko Nagurski," he said, "and I can assure you Bronko never threw ones that hard."

Johnson cackles at the memories. "I'd flip guys in the air, knock them off their feet, boom!"

Johnson was also a Pro Bowl defensive back, and was so tough that the 49ers sometimes played him at middle guard. He moved on to Detroit and Pittsburgh, where he served as bodyguard to quarterback Bobby Layne and finally got a chance to run more. He ran for 1,141 yards in 1962—only three players in history had gained more at the time—and 1,048 in 1964.

"John could do everything—run or catch or block," said Dick Hoak, who played halfback for the Steelers then and has been their backfield coach ever since. "He was as good a blocker as I've ever seen. Touching John was like leaning against a cement wall. Your hand never moved. Jim Brown was like that, only Jim Brown never blocked anybody."

Maybe not, but he sure ran over everybody.

Andy Russell, then a Pittsburgh rookie, remembers the defense watching a film of Brown running for 232 yards and 2 touchdowns versus Dallas in 1963.

"He ran through the line," Russell said, "and six guys jumped on him. Six! You couldn't even see Brown, and then all of sudden you saw the mound moving downfield. Our coach stopped the camera. He wouldn't let us see what happened: people started falling off the mound, and Brown broke away for a [71-yard] touchdown.

"So [coach] Buddy Parker said, 'OK, here's the game plan. He's so dangerous, I want you to let him run free for three quarters. My theory is, by the fourth quarter, he'll be so tired, maybe we can stop him then. We're still in the race, and I don't want him to hurt any of you.' I'm a rookie and I'm thinking, 'What the hell is this strategy?' He was trying to humiliate us. In practice, he put a guy wearing 32 in a red shirt, meaning we were never allowed to touch him. Then, right before the game, he said, 'The first guy who tackles Jim Brown will be fined. I don't want anyone getting hurt.'

"Well, we had a real good day against him, held him to 99 yards. We won the game 9–7, and the winning points were for a safety when we tackled Jim Brown in the end zone. They were backed up on the 1. They were so confident in him, they ran a quick pitch to him instead of a quarterback sneak or the fullback up the middle. You don't call a blitz in that situation, but our coaches did. So Bob Schmitz comes free on the blitz and hits Brown dead-center perfect just as he catches the pitch. Brown doesn't go down. Two, three, four, five guys hit him, and he never stops moving forward. I think the officials finally blew the whistle just so he wouldn't embarrass us. That was about the only tackle Schmitz made all day, and he was voted NFL Player of the Week."

Jim Taylor had the misfortune of playing fullback for the star-studded Green Bay Packers at the same time Brown played for Cleveland, so Taylor was always considered the second-best fullback of the sixties. But he was one tough fullback, the only other player to lead the league in rushing during Brown's tenure. He was the 1962 NFL Player of the Year with a career-high 1,474 yards—one of five straight 1,000-yard seasons—and retired second only to Brown in rushing yards.

"Jim Brown will give you that leg and then take it away from you," coach Vince Lombardi said. "Jim Taylor will give it to you and then ram in through your chest!"

The seventies were dominated by Larry Csonka, the ramrod for the Miami Dolphins' back-to-back titles. He bulled for 112 yards in Super Bowl VII to cap the NFL's only unbeaten season and bashed for a then-record 145 yards and 2 scores as MVP of Super Bowl VIII. Zonk, who played in the AFL, WFL, and NFL, ran for more than 8,000 yards and 400 points, and fumbled just once in every 95 touches. Often called "the Bronko Nagurski of the 1970s," he played despite a cracked eardrum, several concussions, and at least a dozen broken noses.

Considering his crazy antics, some people thought John Riggins got hit in the head once too often. Riggo broke most of Gale Sayers' college rushing records at Kansas. When he was inducted into the Football Hall

Daryl Johnston is the nineties version of an old-fashioned fullback—a devastating lead blocker for Emmitt Smith and a fine receiver for Troy Aikman, as well as a runner.

of Fame in 1992, he ranked third in touchdowns, sixth in rushing, and ninth in combined yards. He broke Csonka's Super Bowl mark with 166 yards in Super Bowl XVII, including a 43-yard winning TD in the fourth quarter, after which he proclaimed, "Ron [Reagan] may be president, but tonight, I'm the king!"

Earl Campbell turned the Houston Oilers into Earlers—and winners. "He may not be in a class all by himself," coach Bum Phillips said, "but it doesn't take long to call the roll." A one-man demolition derby, he led the league in rushing each of his first three seasons, capped by 1,934 yards in 1980, the third-highest total in history, and averaged a whopping 1,176 yards in eight pro seasons.

Trying to tackle him, Cincinnati defensive end Gary Burley said, was like "standing blindfolded in the middle of I-75, dodging the cars, and trying to tackle the biggest truck out there."

CHAPTER THREE
THE ELUDERS

The great runners leave defenders with little choice, really. It's like this: How do you want to die? Do you want to be run over by a diesel truck? Or left naked, out in the cold, with thousands looking on and laughing?

"I always liked guys who tried to run right over you—the Larry Csonkas, the Jim Taylors," seven-time Pro Bowl linebacker Andy Russell said. "You liked them because they didn't humiliate you. You'd figure, 'He might have knocked me over, but at least I grabbed on.' It's really humiliating when you just come up with air. The Mercury Morrises and the O.J. Simpsons could make you miss."

They could make you look silly.

They could take your breath away.

Simpson was the NFL's first 2,000-yard runner. Morris, the lightning to Csonka's thunder, is one of only three men to carry at least 750 times and average 5 yards a crack. The immortal Jim Brown and Gale Sayers are the others.

Not all the Eluders are famous. Like Sayers, some are shooting stars.

"Willie Gallimore would definitely be in your all-time elusives, along with Dickie Post," NFL Films president Steve Sabol said. "Because of our film library, I've had the opportunity to see a lot of great running backs who are totally ignored today. Willie Gallimore didn't play long enough in the NFL, but when you watch the runs he made, you think of Gale Sayers and Barry Sanders. He was put up for the Hall of Fame a couple of years ago, yet because he didn't play very long and didn't play for a good Bears team, he's forgotten. I did a film on him, and that film is really something. He was really an incredible runner."

Barry Sanders, racing 85 yards en route to a typical 166-yard day at Tampa Bay in 1994, is "the best back in football," proclaims Jerry Glanville, the coach turned commentator. "This guy will make nine people miss just to make a yard."

Gale Sayers' career was shortened by knee injuries, but no one who saw him run will ever forget his hummingbird quickness.

Sabol did another film featuring, among others, Post, a stumpy little waterbug for the San Diego Chargers in the old AFL, and Jon Arnett, a jitterbug for the Los Angeles Rams. Jaguar Jon never was a full-time halfback, but he was such a spectacular spot player as a runner, receiver, and returner that he went to five straight Pro Bowls. He was a breathtaking runner, like another West Coast back of that era, Hall of Famer Hugh McElhenny, a.k.a. the King.

"I was good at dodgeball and all those games you play when you're young," Arnett told NFL Films. "It's just something you do out of instinct. There are a lot of average backs that have to think about it. You can ask them why they cut and they'll say, 'Well, I planted my foot and I saw the guy coming.' You ask the great backs why, and they hardly remember it. They just cut because they saw something. Style, that's you."

Gale Sayers embodied style. Ask George Young, the Giants general manager and a longtime football man, to name the greatest run he ever saw and he names a Sayers touchdown of about 65 yards against the Colts. "He ran a sweep to the right and in some magical way, he cut at a 90-degree angle at full speed and ran into the end zone. It wasn't complicated, but I've never seen anybody cut at the speed he cut at and then accelerate off it. When you see pictures of him, you always see that picture."

Then there was a run against the Packers following his knee surgery. Sayers headed right, found the Packers had strung out the play, cut between two, faked a third and a fourth to the ground, put his hand down to regain his balance while going back across the field, and immediately cut straight upfield to make another Packer miss. Two Packers finally grabbed on, and he carried them 5 yards before they brought him down.

The Kansas Comet had thighs almost as thick and strong as Jim Brown's, but quicker feet. He was as elusive as Sanders, but a better inside runner, blocker, receiver, and returner. He was poetry and grace, unforgettable and unmistakable.

O.J. was a unique blend of size, strength, shiftiness, and speed. Watch him on videotape and it seems like the tape is playing tricks with your eyes, as if he's on fast-forward and everyone else is going normal speed.

"He got our fastest guy, Lemar Parrish, one-on-one, and he made poor Lemar look like he was standing there," ex-Bengals All-Pro Mike Reid said, shaking his head in amazement. "Lemar even came back to the huddle kind of giggling and looked at us and asked, 'What do you guys expect?'"

Once, the Colts defense bunched in front of O.J., but O.J. somehow squeezed through a hole that nobody else could see, only to find a Colt squared up in front of him. O.J. sliced inside, and all the Colt could do was get an arm on him. Two other Colts ran alongside him momentarily—until he simply blew by them. Another had the angle on him for the sideline and he cut back, turned the guy around—a full 180—and the guy still had a yard on him, but it didn't matter. The Juice was loose! Touchdown!

Playing for the Bills, Simpson once caught an 8-yard flip over the middle at the Miami 47, turned, found a linebacker in his face and made an incredible cut, and all the 'backer could do was just wave good-bye. Two Dolphins greeted him. One missed. The other buried his head in O.J.'s numbers, but O.J. knocked him rolling back onto his keister, made a 90-degree cut past another Dolphin, stutter-stepped and cut back outside to avoid another, picked up some blockers—they knew he could take any play all the way, so they were hustling to block 30 yards downfield—and went by two more Dolphins before two more finally brought him down at the 10.

Walter Payton said his finest run came as a rookie in December 1975. Almost as soon as he got the handoff, a Saint dived at his legs, and he jumped over him, stopped as another Saint hit him, carried him left until he broke the tackle, headed back to the right, and shucked another tackle. "Then I said, 'Well, I gotta start going forward,'" Payton recalled. He was finally able to turn the corner, run by a linebacker, split two defenders, and race down the sideline before three Saints hemmed him in. No

Walter Payton concluded his career after this January 10, 1988, playoff game against the Redskins as the leading ground gainer in NFL history.

ABOVE: Green Bay held Barry Sanders in check 2 of the 3 games they played in 1994. But he's "still the scariest running back in the league," said defensive lineman Reggie White.

OPPOSITE: Buffalo had no prettier sight than O.J. Simpson taking a pitchout or sweep around right end, as he does here against Cleveland's Joe Jones.

on him. Then the Chiefs appeared to have trapped him along the left sideline and he flinched, crouched, and broke a tackle with a Chief tugging on his face mask. Two more Chiefs reached and missed. Another hit him; Payton lowered his head and a big pileup ensued. Don't ask how, but he managed to get out of it. Another Chief lowered his head, and Payton knocked the guy down. More Chiefs grabbed at his legs and he shucked them all. He went around yet another Chief before the final defender between Payton and the goal line grabbed onto his waist, slipped down those powerful, churning thighs, and dragged him down. Finally.

Barry Sanders, the most elusive back today, is not only slippery, but strong, too. All-Pro defensive tackle Keith Millard could bench-press unbelievable amounts and outweighed Sanders by 60 pounds, and couldn't believe Sanders could break his tackle. "Amazing," Millard said.

Once against Miami, the Lions needed a first down to assure a victory. Sanders went airborne, but halfway over the pile, 226-pound Louis Oliver met him head-on and sent him catapulting back whence he came. Sanders somehow landed on his feet and instantaneously knifed through the line for 3 yards and the win.

"He what?" Oliver asked, still not believing what had happened afterward.

"No. 20 defied a lot of laws of physics and gravity," Bills Pro Bowl linebacker Darryl Talley said after another magic act. "He made us look foolish. Biscuit [All-Pro Cornelius Bennett] locked him in his arms. I saw Barry's helmet hit the ground, and what does he do? He bounces off his helmet, holds his body off the ground, spins around on his hand, and runs the other way. How does he do that?"

matter. He stopped, picked up two blockers, and zoomed past the last Saint.

Payton's old boss, Bill Tobin, will never forget Sweetness' run against the Chiefs in Soldier Field. "I don't know if it was his best one," Tobin said, "but it was one that was unbelievable." Payton spun away from one Chief to find two linebackers square in front of him. He spun past one, and the other could only get an arm

But often, Sanders just leaves them speechless. Mitch Albom, who sees him all the time as a *Detroit Free Press* columnist, wrote of the ESPN rehearsal where a bunch of football's finest ex-jocks and commentators watched a tape of Sanders: "And when the tape ended, we couldn't help it, we were giggling. Those were our comments. Grown men. Giggling."

CHAPTER FOUR

STARS OF TOMORROW

Ted Marchibroda played with Ollie Matson, a Hall of Fame running back and Olympic gold medal sprinter. He has coached Walter Payton, Thurman Thomas, Billy Sims, Larry Brown, Joe Washington, and Lydell Mitchell. But already, the Colts coach ranks Marshall Faulk with the very best of them.

"He goes faster, quicker than anybody I've ever seen," said Marchibroda. "Not just from a standing start but the ability to dart and come to a complete stop, then go full speed again almost immediately.

"He's faster than Thurman Thomas; that puts him over Thurman. Larry Brown was MVP in 1972 when I was in Washington; he was strong and tough, but Marshall has more overall ability. Sims was a great runner…but Marshall is quicker, more of a darter, with Sims' breakaway speed.…He's probably faster than Barry Sanders. Barry has more strength in his legs, but Marshall has strength in his legs, too. As a runner, you might take Barry first, but add Marshall's catching ability, his running pass routes, and I think he equals Barry. He has great hands; I don't think he dropped a ball all year. He will stick his nose in when called upon [to block]. And one of the things we forget to mention is that he's durable; he played every game as a rookie."

And what a rookie year he had. ESPN's Mike Patrick likened him to Sanders because of his speed and moves. Broadcast partner Joe Theismann said Faulk reminded him of Tony Dorsett because he goes from 0 to 60 so fast. Equally fast was his impact on the Colts' running game. After finishing last or next to last in rushing offense four years in a row, they zoomed to fourth in the first year of the Marshall Plan. After scoring only 4 rushing touchdowns in 1993, they had 15 in 1994. After running for 100 yards as a team in only 10 games in the 1990s, they had a dozen 100-yard games in 1994 and also doubled their victory total.

Only Sanders accounted for a larger percentage of his team's total yards than Faulk. Only three rookies in NFL history had more scrimmage yards (rushing and receiving yards combined). Only ten ever had more rushing yards. Only Eric Dickerson ever had more rushing yards, scrimmage yards, or a higher percentage of the Colts offense.

A runaway choice as Rookie of the Year or Offensive Rookie of the Year in every poll in existence, Faulk was the lone rookie in the Pro Bowl (where he did not dissapoint, recording 180 yards in the game).

Colts boss Bill Tobin, a brilliant draft scout for the Bears, thinks it premature to compare Faulk with Payton, who stood the test of time and became what Tobin considers the best all-around back in history. Payton was certainly tougher as well as a better blocker, but Tobin can't help noting that Faulk is the same size as Payton, and whereas Payton covered 40 yards in 4.55 to 4.6 seconds, Faulk does it in 4.3 seconds.

"He's got one thing that some of the greatest running backs of all time do not have," Tobin said. "Some of the greatest had good speed, even excellent speed; this kid has exceptional speed. O.J. might have been a 4.3. Bo Jackson was, but he never really did it in our

Marshall Faulk made an instant impact as a rookie, running for 143 yards and 3 scores in his debut. Shown here in his next game, Faulk gained 104 yards rushing and 82 receiving despite a sprained left wrist.

league. Dickerson had it. They might be the only other ones. The other thing Marshall has is great eyes and anticipation. He can change directions instantaneously with what his eyes see. Most great backs have great eyes and they let their instincts take over. They don't know how they do things. I've talked to Walter about it. Sometimes, they watch films and say, 'Hmm, man! I did that?' It's not preplanned, like a lot of other positions. It's God-given, just instinctive."

Can Faulk take those talents into the next millennium? Can he become one of the all-time greats? Bucko Kilroy, who's been playing, coaching, or scouting in the NFL since 1943, said he already considers him among the best.

Faulk was drafted second in 1994. The other back voted Most Likely to Succeed, Ki-Jana Carter, was chosen first in 1995. Carter's new coach, David Shula, said he has the vision, patience, strength, and power of Emmitt Smith, but with a lot more speed.

Shula has reason to be biased, but Tony Razzano doesn't. The longtime scouting guru—he helped build the 49ers into the team of the eighties (and maybe the nineties)—calls Carter the best back he's seen in thirty-five years. Better than Payton, Smith, Sanders, O.J., and all the rest.

Carter combines rare athleticism—he ran a 4.38 40-yard dash and jumped 39 inches from a standing start

Rashaan Salaam, the 1994 Heisman Trophy winner, became a pro starter at age twenty and promptly led the 1995 Chicago Bears in rushing.

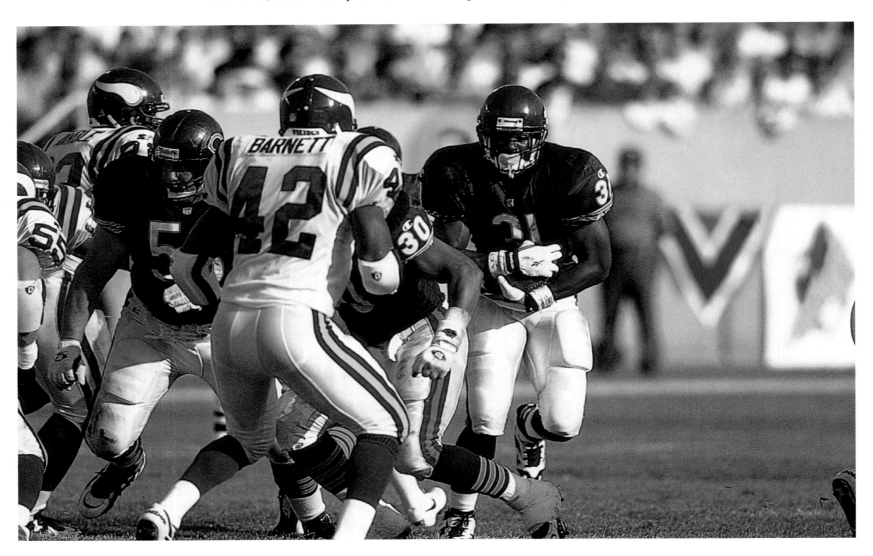

at 225 pounds—with rare instincts. He can slash for tough yards inside or turn the corner with ease. He averaged a remarkable 7.8 yards per carry while running for 1,539 yards and 23 touchdowns for the 1994 Penn State Nittany Lions.

Faulk and Carter may be the brightest but are hardly the only stars of tomorrow.

Rashaan Salaam blew away Carter in the Heisman balloting. Buoyed by an extra 100 carries, he joined Marcus Allen, Mike Rozier, and Barry Sanders as the only backs to gain 2,000 yards in a single college season. All three became Pro Bowlers, and Allen and Sanders both won NFL rushing titles. But the pros won-

der if Salaam has the speed and elusiveness to be great. That's why four backs and twenty players were chosen before the Bears snagged him.

The question about Tyrone Wheatley is: can he stay healthy? He ran for 4,178 yards and 47 touchdowns in his four years at Michigan while missing just 5 games. "If that's not durable enough for you, what is?" Wheatley asked. "This question bugs me a lot."

Wheatley runs the 40 in 4.4 seconds at 230 pounds, and if you saw him in the 1993 Rose Bowl, you know he could be a great one for the Giants. Averaging a stunning 15.7 yards per carry, he ran for 235 yards in that game, including touchdown runs of 56, 88, and 24 yards.

ABOVE LEFT: **Tyrone Wheatley flashed his potential as the Giants' number one pick in 1995.**

ABOVE RIGHT: **Seattle's Chris Warren has run for 1,000 yards in four consecutive seasons despite being just a fourth-round pick.**

ABOVE LEFT: **Ricky Watters has proven to be a 1,000-yard runner for both the 49ers and Eagles.**

ABOVE RIGHT: **Curtis Martin wasn't a high draft pick, but the Patriots have high hopes for him in the immediate future.**

OPPOSITE: **Jerome Bettis has been an effective bulldozing back for the Rams.**

But you can get slighted in the draft a lot worse than Salaam and Wheatley did and still turn out to be a terrific back. Terrell Davis wasn't chosen until the sixth round in 1995, after 195 other players, but he set all kinds of records. He became the first Denver rookie running back to start the opener since Floyd Little in 1966. He became the lowest-drafted player to run for 1,000 yards as a rookie. And with 135 yards against the Cardinals, he ran for more yards in Mile High Stadium than any Bronco in two decades.

Curtis Martin wasn't chosen until the third round in 1995, but he ran for 102 yards and the winning touch-down in the final seconds of his pro debut, and he was an immediate impact player for the New England Patriots. He became the first rookie since Barry Sanders to top 1,000 yards in his first dozen games, in which the Patriots were 5-0 when he ran for 100 yards and 0-7 when he did not.

The pros had worried about Martin's durability, but he proved to be workhorse for the Patriots and "amazed me with his tremendous stamina" coach Parcells said. "It's an ingredient all great players have."

Chris Warren was a fourth-round pick from a small Division III school, Ferrum College, with just 17 carries and 24 yards his first two pro seasons with the Seattle Seahawks. But when finally given the ball, he exploded with four consecutive 1,000-yard seasons. And talk about gritty—he ran for a career-high 185 yards just a week and a half after breaking two ribs in an auto accident. He also broke the Pro Bowl rushing record of the immortal O.J., but only for about thirty seconds, when Faulk ran by them both for the record.

Five forgettable running backs and forty-four players overall were drafted ahead of Ricky Watters, and he missed his rookie season with a broken foot. But he blossomed into perhaps the league's best running-receiving threat in three years for the 49ers, capped by a record-tying 3 touchdowns in Super Bowl XXIX. The 1995 Eagles gave him a chance to run even more and he had his best year yet.

If you're looking for a big back, Natrone Means is your man. He's so good that he earned two nicknames in two years: Natrone Means Business and Natrone Bomb. He's equal parts brahma bull and ballerina. "He's big, fast and he'll make you miss as often as he runs over you," Steelers safety Darren Perry said.

Means has studied the styles of both Payton and Earl Campbell. A five-foot-ten-inch, 245-pound load, he doesn't run quite as hard as Campbell, but close enough. He doesn't have all of Payton's moves, but he can do a 180-degree spin and leave defenders grabbing air. In 1994, his first year as a starter, he led San Diego to the Super Bowl, broke Chargers records for rushing yards and attempts, and ran for more yards than any back save Sanders, Warren, and Smith.

The Battering Ram, Jerome Bettis, ran for 1,000 yards each of his first two seasons. Then-teammate Irv Eatman put it best: "Anything as big and fast as Bettis usually comes equipped with a catalytic converter. Bettis has the power of a Dodge Ram but the speed of a Maserati." Bettis beat Rick Mirer to become 1993's Rookie of the Year and beat Thomas and Sanders to become first-team All-Pro. He nearly beat out Smith for the NFL rushing title even though he only started 1 of the Rams' first 5 games.

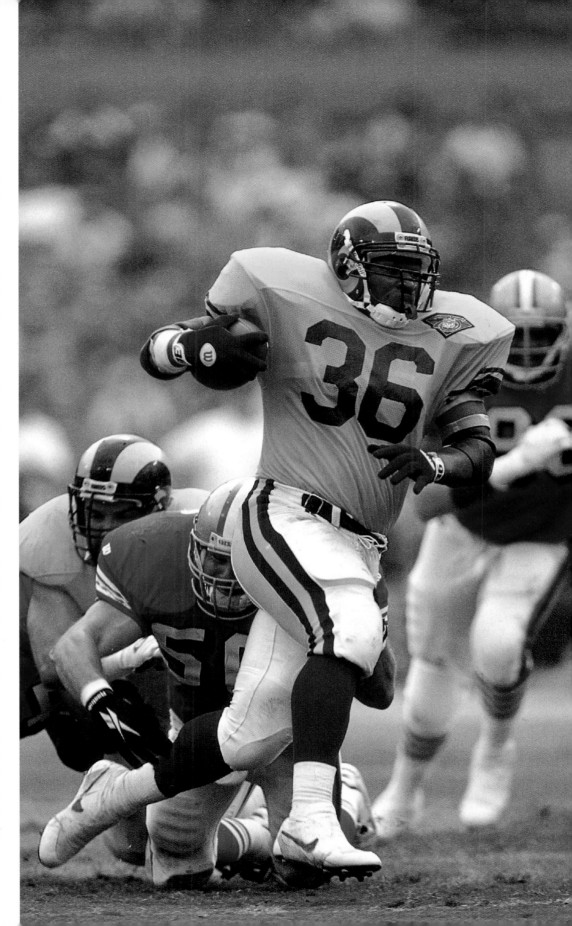

CHAPTER FIVE

THE GREATEST RUNNING BACKS OF ALL TIME

To determine the best backs in history, one must consider who were the greats of each era, who were the toughest, who were the most elusive, and who were the most complete. But when you talk about the most gifted athletes in a sport that spans nearly eight decades, some great players are bound to be left out.

"I've done enough films and lists," said NFL Films president Steve Sabol, "that you know you haven't done your research unless you get at least ten irate letters and people moaning, 'How could you leave this person off? Do you think you know what you're talking about?'"

Marcus Allen is one player who ultimately missed the cut because he doesn't have the speed to wow fans and doesn't do one thing better than anyone else. But like Walter Payton, he does everything well. As Allen enters the 1996 season, he is second in catches by a running back, with 549, and tied for second with Walter Payton in career touchdowns, with 125, one shy of Jim Brown. He is third in combined yards—having passed James Brooks, Eric Dickerson, and Jim Brown in 1995—and is eighth in career rushing yards. He is the only player ever to gain both 10,000 yards rushing and 5,000 yards receiving.

One thing Allen has is longevity. He is one of only a small handful of backs to survive fourteen seasons. He's a clutch player, a 100-yard runner in 5 postseason games, and MVP of Super Bowl XVIII and the 1985 regular season. And no talented runner in the eighties and nineties was a better blocker.

"To me," said Sabol, "a lot of times it's not how many yards a person gains, but how many they gain in meaningful situations. Marcus Allen is one of great all-time goal-line backs. He's like Paul Hornung was. You get him near the goal line or third-and-four, he is really special in that situation. Another point that I might bring up about Marcus Allen is that we just interviewed about fifteen current running backs about the greatest run they ever saw, and the run that got the most votes was Marcus Allen's run in the Super Bowl against the Redskins. Marcus was a great blocker, a tremendous pass receiver, a slashing runner."

Marcus Allen leaves three Redskins in his wake as he breaks away for what still stands as the longest TD run in Super Bowl history. That 74-yard gain helped him to a then-record 191 yards rushing and the MVP Award, and contributed to the Raiders romp, 38–9, in Super Bowl XVIII.

Giants General Manager George Young suggests another omission: "Lenny Moore was multitalented. He could catch as well as any flanker. He was as fluid a back as you could find. You could line him up in the backfield or out wide as a receiver and he was brutal. He was a tall, lean guy who just did everything easy, one of the more graceful runners."

Indeed, it could be easily justified that Moore deserves a spot in any top twenty. He scored more touchdowns than all but five men in professional football history, averaging a remarkable 16.6 yards per catch and 4.8 per carry. He was All-NFL five times and both Player of the Year and Comeback Player of the Year in 1964, when he scored a record 20 touchdowns. From late 1963 until early 1965, he scored TDs in 18 straight games, still a record. He even threw 2 touchdown passes and returned a kick for another during his Hall of Fame career.

Lineman Jim Parker said Moore "was so smooth, that he could lay his feet down and walk on eggs without breaking them." Another teammate, Carl Taseff, compared him to "a symphony on the football field."

"Lenny Moore was one of the first modern backs to catch passes and run," Sabol said. "He was the precursor of Roger Craig. He had the most incredible knee action I've ever seen. One of the single greatest runs in our film library was a run he had in 1965 against the Packers, where he ran through seven tacklers, all trying to tackle him around the knees. He was a real game-breaker. In one of our scripts, I wrote, 'He was lightning in a game long ruled by thunder.'"

Go back to the gridiron's pioneer years, and you'll also find true sixty-minute men in the Hall of Fame such as "Bullet" Bill Dudley, Cliff Battles, Tony Canadeo, Joe Guyon, Clarke Hinkle, Tuffy Leemans, George "One-Play" McAfee, Johnny "Blood" McNally, and Ken Strong.

RIGHT: **James Brooks was a short little scatback, but incredibly tough. He retired as one of the top five in combined yards, ahead of much more famous players.**

OPPOSITE: **Charley Trippi's name isn't in the record books, but he was the epitome of the do-it-all players of football's growing years, excelling as a runner, receiver, passer, defensive back, and return man.**

Move to the postwar era, and you'll find a slew of complete backs, beginning with Charley Trippi, who ran for 206 yards on 14 carries, 102 of those in the 1947 NFL championship game on 2 punt returns. The biggest star in the Chicago Cardinals' "Dream Backfield," he not only averaged 5.1 yards per carry and 10.2 per catch, he started at quarterback for two seasons and defensive back for another two. The Hall of Famer also averaged 40.4 yards per punt, 13.7 per punt return, and 22.1 per kick return.

Ollie Matson was called "The Messiah" when he signed with the 1952 Cardinals. He was 220 pounds of power and speed and was the winner of gold and bronze medals in the 1952 Olympics. He played seven years and still had so much left to give that the Rams had to trade nine players to get him. He played on such bad teams that it seemed that every opponent concentrated on him, yet he still managed to gain 12,884 yards and score 40 times as a runner, 23 as a receiver, and 9 as a returner. He even completed 5 passes and intercepted 3 others.

Doak Walker didn't last as long because he found he could make more money selling insurance. But the 1948 Heisman Trophy winner and three-time All-American was a do-it-all Hall of Famer. In little more than five seasons with the Lions, he made the Pro Bowl five times and All-Pro four times. He retired with 534 points, then third in NFL history. He averaged 4.9 yards per carry, 16.7 per catch, 15.8 per punt return, 25.5 per kick return, 30 per interception return, and 39.1 per punt, and even kicked 183 extra points and 49 field goals.

Frank Gifford was the 1956 Player of the Year, the 1962 Comeback Player of the Year, and a 1977 Hall of Fame inductee. He was voted to the Pro Bowl at more positions than anyone else—once as a defensive back, once as a flanker, and five times as a halfback,—and even completed 29 passes for 823 yards and 14 touchdowns.

Paul Hornung might have been the most important player in the Packers' dynasty of the sixties. "The Golden Boy" was lauded for his multiple talents as a runner, receiver, passer, blocker, kicker, and scorer. The bigger the game, the better he played, and thirty-five years later, his 176 points remains the NFL single-season record.

Leroy Kelly was an eighth-round draft pick who carried just 43 times his first two seasons, and though he had led the league in punt returns in 1965, Browns fans feared a huge falloff when Jim Brown retired prematurely and the unknown back from unknown Morgan State took over. As it turned out, Kelly not only had the same number of letters in his last name but the same number of yards in his feet. He averaged 5.5 yards a carry and ran for 1,141 yards and a league-high 15 touchdowns in his first year as a regular. He then won back-to-back rushing titles the next two years, and led the league in scoring with 20 touchdowns in 1968. He retired ranked fourth in both rushing and combined yards.

James Brooks, a tough little scatback for the Chargers and Bengals, retired ranked fifth in combined yards, ahead of such superstars as O.J. Simpson and Franco Harris. Craig, a fearless, high-stepping runner for the great 49ers teams of the 1980s, made the top twenty in combined yards and set a record for receptions by a running back.

Herschel Walker doesn't have the moves or eyes of many of the great backs, and he isn't effective unless he's lining up deep and getting the ball a lot, but his awesome combination of size and speed helped him enter the 1995 season ranked seventh in combined yards. If you add in his three USFL seasons—the NFL doesn't count USFL, WFL, or AAFC but does count AFL stats—he's first in career rushing touchdowns (114), and second in all-time rushing yards (13,684) and first in combined yards (23,062). Even without his USFL statistics, only Payton, Tony Dorsett, Brown, Eric Dickerson, Jerry Rice, and Allen have more combined yards.

Ottis Anderson finished eighth in all-time rushing yards and rushing TDs, and thirteenth in combined yards, but was passed by Marcus Allen in rushing yards

and both Allen and Emmitt Smith in rushing touchdowns. Most people probably remember a slow but tough Super Bowl XXV MVP for the Giants, but O.J. Anderson burst into the NFL as a big, fast slasher who averaged nearly 1,800 yards rushing and receiving his first three years with the Cardinals.

"He's like TNT, he's such an explosive back," Eagles linebacker Jerry Robinson said then. "He's like the Metroliner: once he's gone, he's gone. There's no catching him."

The great running backs, however, have been able to perform year after year: they combine power, elusiveness, and athletic ability to help themselves and their teams reach new heights. The great ones were artists; they carved out football fields with sweeping lines of motion.

OPPOSITE: **Herschel Walker is one of the all-time leaders in combined yards, especially if you count his days in the USFL, when he was most dominant.**

ABOVE: **Ottis "O.J." Anderson was a big, fast game-breaker for some average Cardinals teams before gaining fame as the slow but dependable star of Super Bowl XXV for the Giants.**

JIM BROWN

Sam Huff remembers Jim Brown. All he has to do is look in the mirror and see the scar across his nose. It's a permanent reminder of the day that Jim Brown scarred his nose and shattered his teeth.

"I woke up on the trainer's table," Huff said.

"Woke up" is a common phrase in Jim Brown stories. Traditionally, defenders are supposed to dole out punishment and runners absorb it, but Jim Brown reversed the equation with frightening consequences.

Another Hall of Famer, Bob Lilly, still remembers the first time he tackled Jim Brown. "I was on the 7 yard line and I was in perfect position to tackle Jim Brown. When I woke up a few minutes later, my face mask was creased on my face and he'd scored a touchdown."

A seven-time Pro Bowler, Andy Russell, remembers his first meeting, too. "My rookie year with the Steelers, we were number one versus the run, and Jim Brown was leading the league in running. Classic matchup, right? First series, we kicked off and they had 80 yards to go. First play, Brown went through the middle of the line, ran over Myron Pottios, who was a heck of a linebacker, a Pro Bowler, and went 20 yards. The next play, he went around left end for 50. The next play was from our 10. I was playing left linebacker. I guess playing in the NFL wasn't a big enough challenge for Jim Brown; he had to tell you where he was going. He really tipped off what he was doing. So I said to our left end, Lou Michaels, `It's a quick pitch, let's play it.' Lou knocked off the blocker and I had a clear shot at Jim Brown.

"I did everything right: hit him in the numbers, caught him with a rising blow, wrapped my arms, had my legs driving. There was a bright flash of light, a bright explosion I never saw before. And when I woke up, I was lying on my back in the end zone, and he was saying, 'Hey, kid, you can let go of my shoe now.'"

Another astonishing run is featured in an NFL Films video, *The Great Ones*. A linebacker blitzes into the backfield untouched and meets Brown head-on just as he takes his first step. The linebacker has all the momentum, and Brown has no time to react. He just flicks out his forearm and knocks off the linebacker's helmet and drops him on his back!

But he's not done. He spins, heads toward the opposite sideline, runs by one guy, a second, a third, a fourth, and, now in the open field, a fifth. One last defender tries to grab his shoulders at the 5, and Brown carries him into the end zone before depositing him on his back.

In a nutshell, Brown had power, size, and speed. "He was six-foot-three inches, 232 pounds, and he beat Bobby Mitchell in the 40-yard dash, and Mitchell was the coholder of the dash record," marveled Floyd Peters, a former teammate and longtime NFL assistant coach. Peters and almost everyone who ever played or coached with or against Brown—including Huff, Russell, Ray Nitschke, Joe Schmidt, Frank Gifford, Willie Davis, Pat Summerall, Paul Brown, George Young, Ted Marchibroda, and Gale Sayers—insist he's the greatest ever. A few experts, such as Steve Sabol and Colts boss Bill Tobin, nominate Walter Payton as the best all-around back because Brown rarely blocked.

"Jimmy Brown didn't even try to block, and I still think he's the greatest back ever," said Ray Mansfield. "I've never seen anybody like him. You dreaded playing him. He'd work the whole team over. It seemed like he was a robot.

"I hit him a couple of times, and the world seemed to explode. I hit him going full speed once, and I swear to this day that I wrapped my arm around him and pulled him down, but in the film, I just bounced like I hit a bus and he ran 62 yards for a touchdown."

Brown led the league in rushing eight of his nine seasons. In 1962, the only year he didn't win the rushing title, he still gained 996 yards with a wrist that was announced as sprained but might have been broken. During his career, he averaged 104.3 rushing yards and 1.07 touchdowns per game, topping 100 yards in 58 of

118 games. He would have put every rushing record out of sight if he hadn't retired at age thirty for the movies.

Yet many of his records are still intact. Nobody else has won more than four rushing titles, and nobody has averaged more than his 5.2 yards a carry. Brown's records that have been broken had stood for many years. His single-season rushing record of 1,864 yards remained intact until 1973, when it was broken by O.J. Simpson. His 12,312 career yards record stood until Walter Payton broke it in 1984. And his record of 126 touchdowns wasn't beaten until 1994, by Jerry Rice.

Ironically, Jim Brown might not have ended up with the Cleveland Browns if coach Paul Brown had been able to get the draft pick he wanted. Ed Kiely, part of the Pittsburgh Steelers contingent at the 1957 college draft, remembers choosing quaterback Len Dawson just ahead of the Browns.

"Cleveland was at the table right near us," Kiely said, "and Paul Brown knocked his fist on the table and knocked some books off it. He was so upset because he wanted Dawson. So after a lull, Paul went back to his books. And his pick was Jim Brown."

Jim Brown topped 100 yards in nearly half his pro starts and set rushing records that remained out of sight for years. Some have fallen now, but nobody would have caught him if he had not retired prematurely at thirty to pursue acting. If Brown had played until the natural end of his athletic career, He might have reached 20,000 yards and 150 touchdowns.

ERIC DICKERSON

Eric Dickerson had not only rare speed and quickness for a big back, but excellent eyes and instincts. "The difference between a great back and a good back is the great backs can see the seam and know when to cut against the grain," Steve Sabol said. "Marcus Allen can do it. Dickerson could do it."

Look in the NFL record books, and you'll see Eric Dickerson's name above or beside all the legends.

Nobody else ever ran for 2,105 yards in a season.

Nobody else ever ran for 1,808 yards or 18 touchdowns as a rookie.

Nobody else ever had more 100-yard games in a single season (12).

Nobody else ever ran for more yards in a playoff game (248).

Only Barry Sanders had as many consecutive 1,000-yard seasons (seven). Only Walter Payton (16,726) ran for more career yards (13,259). Only Payton (77) had more career 100-yard games (64). Only Jim Brown (8) had more rushing titles (4). And only Brown, O.J. Simpson, and Earl Campbell had more 200-yard games (3).

Yet Dickerson also led the league in *buts*.

"Dickerson has the numbers," Giants general manager George Young said. "But he doesn't have any championships, does he?"

He was a sleek slasher, reminiscent of O.J. Simpson, only faster.

"But he didn't seem to be as dedicated," ex-Steeler Ray Mansfield said. "That separates guys that could have been and guys that were."

He was six-foot-three and 225 pounds, with world-class speed. He was a graceful prototype who could flash inside or turn the corner like O.J.

"Except O.J. was tougher," Steve Sabol said.

If the hole wasn't where it was supposed to be, he could spot a seam, cut back, and run to daylight. He ranks in the top ten in rushing touchdowns.

But with his swinging arms and upright running style, he also fumbled a whopping seventy-eight times. In the 1985 NFC title game, Chicago defensive coordinator Buddy Ryan vowed that the Bears would force Dickerson to fumble three times. "They can try to strip me if they want," Dickerson replied, "but if they try to strip and miss, I'll be in the secondary and it will be a long day for them."

It was a long day, only for Dickerson. He gained only 46 yards and fumbled twice. The Rams lost 24–0 and never made it to a championship game again during Dickerson's years there.

Dickerson might have broken all the records if he'd stayed in Los Angeles, where his coach, John Robinson, adored him and played him at tailback. He gained 1,800 yards or more in three of his first four seasons. And yes, those were 16-game seasons, not the 12 or 14 games that Brown played, but Dickerson reached 10,000 yards in 91 games, 7 games faster than Brown or anyone else.

"Eric Dickerson could have been outstanding if he had kept his head on straight," Gale Sayers said.

But his head was often elsewhere. Rams fans started calling him "Eric Dollarsign" in Los Angeles when he demanded his second renegotiation in three years in 1987, forcing a trade that involved three teams, four players, and six high draft picks. The Rams still haven't recovered from the trade, the deal eventually proved unrewarding for the Colts as well.

Dickerson gave the Indianapolis team instant credibility. The Colts had gone 38-98-1 the previous decade and had become a national punchline. Even their own fans called them the Dolts and wore paper bags on their heads. With their new goggled superstar, they won 6 of 9 games and the AFC East title. Dickerson led the league in rushing in 1988 and finished third in 1989. But the Colts missed the playoffs both years, and soon, Dickerson yearned to leave the cornfields and speedway of Indiana for his old Malibu mansion and the Hollywood glitterati. After two dismal seasons in which he was slowed by injuries, he was suspended twice for bad behavior and became a cancer with his constant complaints. The Colts finally dumped him on the Raiders, who were looking to revive another renegade. He was so eager to live in Los Angeles that he agreed to a 50 percent cut in his salary.

"He wanted to be a Hollywood boy, so we sent him back to Hollywood," Colts owner Bob Irsay said.

A shadow of his former speed-demon days, Dickerson spent a year in Los Angeles and played a few games in Atlanta before a neck injury forced him to retire. It was a disappointing ending to what could have been a legendary career.

"Dickerson is an interesting case because he really isn't respected at all because he fumbled in big games, because he was a whiner and a crybaby who never made his team better," Sabol said. "I go back to that playoff game in 1985 when Buddy Ryan said we're going to have him put the ball on the ground and he fumbled 2 times. There was a sort of selfishness about him, but that shouldn't diminish his pure ability as a runner."

However, many feel he's worthy of reexamination. When asked who he thought was the greatest runner he'd ever seen, Ricky Watters said "Eric Dickerson. You have to put him in there for his records and statistics."

"They can say what they want to say," Dickerson said, "but I've got the stats to back it up."

TONY DORSETT

Even if it were first and 99 yards to go, the Dallas Cowboys would be in scoring position if Tony Dorsett were in their backfield.

Sounds like hyperbole, but it isn't.

T.D. proved it in the final game of the 1982 season, on Monday Night Football, with the whole nation watching. The Minnesota Vikings backed Dallas to its own 1 yard line and Dorsett to his own end zone.

No matter. T.D. turned a safe, simple plunge up the middle into a work of art and, in the process, made history. Dorsett zoomed through the line, but four Vikings still surrounded him and seemed certain to stop him. Dorsett faked out one on his left and made an incredible cut past another on his right. Two defenders remained, and both had an angle on him, but he used a blocker to shield them and, using his speed, blew by both of them and was gone, running 99 yards for a touchdown.

It is a record that never has been matched and will most likely never be broken.

Tony Dorsett was a crafty back with electrifying moves. Here he finds a hole in the San Diego Chargers' defense.

And you know what? He didn't even need a full complement of Cowboys to do it; Dallas was a man short on that play.

Dorsett left the University of Pittsburgh as the Heisman Trophy winner, a four-time All-American, the first collegian with four 1,000-yard and three 1,500-yard seasons, and owner of fourteen NCAA records.

He left the NFL as a Hall of Famer, a four-time Pro Bowler, the first pro to run for 1,000 yards in each of his first five seasons, and second only to Walter Payton in rushing and combined yards. Only Payton (ten) had more 1,000-yard seasons than Dorsett (eight). In fact, T.D. topped 1,000 yards in fourteen of his first fifteen high school, college, and pro seasons, coming up short only when a strike reduced 1982 to 9 games.

Over the years, all Dorsett ever lost was sleep. He ran the 40 in 4.45 seconds as a rookie and in 4.40 as a thirty-year-old. He was a skinny scatback, just five feet eleven inches and 184 pounds, but missed just 3 games his first nine years. Not until 1987, when he was thirty-three and had both ankles arthroscopically repaired for his "11,000-yard checkup," did he ever slow down. Not until 1989, when his knee "crumbled like a piece of spaghetti" on a "simple, routine play" during preseason practice, was he ever stopped.

He played with a broken wrist, cracked ribs, and even a broken bone in his spinal column in 1985. The last "scared the hell out of me," Dorsett said. "In laymen's terms, it was a broken back." However, the next day, Dorsett ran for 159 yards and eventually accumulated 1,307 that season.

Mostly, Dorsett had a remarkable ability to avoid tacklers and the bruises they brought with them. Early on, he developed a quirky running style with his knees bent loosely to help save them from being twisted and torn. He had phenomenal quickness to get to the hole, waterbug moves when there was no hole, and afterburner speed when he got in the secondary. "I've been

blessed with the God-given talent to somehow pull my arm, leg, and head out of the way to miss the big hits," he said. "There's a degree of luck involved."

And strategy. Many in this macho sport call it unmanly to duck out of bounds to avoid a big hit—Gale Sayers ripped Dorsett and Jim Brown attacked Franco Harris for it—but Dorsett, called it "being smart, not being foolish or crazy."

Not that he wouldn't take on tacklers when necessary. For instance, once against the Rams, he broke 4 tackles before two defenders were finally able to bring him down.

Dorsett averaged only 17 carries a game during his career—which was the main reason he never won a rushing title or drew the acclaim many felt he merited—and sometimes he chafed under Tom Landry's leash. But he also acknowledged there was "probably a good chance" that he wouldn't have lasted as long if he had carried as often as such shooting-star contemporaries as Earl Campbell, Larry Brown, John Brockington, and Wilbert Montgomery. Instead, he achieved "just a remarkable record for a back that's no bigger than he is."

This is remarkable, too: Dallas was able to pick Dorsett second in 1977 after Tampa took Ricky Bell and Seattle took four forgettable picks, which they had obtained in a trade with Dallas.

"Those people in Seattle who made that trade, do they still have their jobs?" Minnesota coach Bud Grant once muttered.

"It's scary," Dorsett said, "to think what might have happened if I'd gone with them."

And it's scary to think what Dorsett might have done if he'd run more.

"If he'd played for the Steelers, with that running game, he'd have broken all kinds of records," Ray Mansfield said. "He was an incredible runner."

Tony Dorsett might have set all kinds of records if Cowboys coach Tom Landry had used him more—then again, the slender scatback might have gotten beaten up and never enjoyed the long career he did. "My philosophy is, he's not that big and he shouldn't take a 30-play pounding every week," Landry said. "So we let him carry twenty times or less each week and it paid off."

RED GRANGE

If the Roaring Twenties really was the golden age of sports, then Red Grange was the golden boy of football. In his time, "The Galloping Ghost" was as popular as Babe Ruth and Jack Dempsey, and his No. 77 was as famous as Michael Jordan's No. 23 is today.

A three-time All-American at Illinois, Grange was the greatest player in college football, which, at the time, dwarfed the embryonic pro league in popularity. Pro football was strictly bush league, played in tawdry tank towns the size of Canton and Kenosha, Rock Island and Racine, Decatur and Duluth. Newspapers didn't cover the games, and even if the teams hand-delivered game stories, they were thrown in the trash or relegated to the bottom of the page. In fact, it was considered unseemly to play for pay.

Times have certainly changed, and it was Red Grange who changed them. He put professional football on the front page, legitimized it, and helped it develop into one of the nation's passions. In a scheme concocted by C.C. Pyle, a former theatrical magician nicknamed "Cash and Carry," Grange debuted for the Chicago Bears on Thanksgiving Day, 1925, just five days after his junior season. The Bears drew thirty-six thousand fans, a record at the time. The Bears then went on a 19-game, coast-to-coast, barnstorming tour, drawing seventy-three thousand fans to New York's Polo Grounds and seventy-five thousand to the Los Angeles Coliseum. *Sports Illustrated* called it "the sixty-six days that made pro football."

But not everyone was ecstatic.

"People don't realize today how the colleges fought against pro ball," Grange said in 1982, eight years before his death at age eighty-seven. "They were afraid the pros would dominate the game. After I signed, my coach at Illinois, Bob Zuppke, wouldn't talk to me for three years. I'd have been more popular with the colleges if I had joined Capone's mob in Chicago rather than the Bears."

Grange's premature departure infuriated college coaches ranging from Amos Alonzo Stagg to Zuppke, who warned Illinois graduate George Halas, the Bears' player-coach and owner, that it could ruin the college game. Halas persuaded the NFL to sign only collegians whose class had graduated.

Still, Halas kept Grange and made about $200,000 from Red's debut, with another $200,000 split between Grange and Pyle. Grange and Pyle also established the first American Football League, in 1926, when the Bears balked at giving Grange a five-figure salary and one-third ownership of the team. The AFL folded after one year, but Grange's New York Yankees joined the NFL in 1927, only to see him suffer a knee injury that forced him to miss the 1928 season and robbed him of much of his elusiveness. Still, when he returned to the Bears in 1929, he remained one of the best defensive backs of his time and a box-office attraction. His achievements included being named All-NFL in 1931, catching the winning pass in the 1932 championship game, and making the game-saving tackle on the last play of the 1933 championship game.

Grange's greatest game, though, was in college in 1924, against a Michigan team that had won 20 in a row. He took the opening kickoff 95 yards for a touchdown, and scored from 67, 54, and 44 yards away, running for a total of 265 yards just in the first quarter. After a five-minute rest, he scored from 13 yards, and later even threw a 20-yard TD. Illinois romped, 39–14, as Grange accounted for 402 yards in forty-one minutes.

Damon Runyon wrote: "He is three or four men rolled into one. He is Jack Dempsey, Babe Ruth, Al Jolson, Paavo Nurmi, and Man o' War."

His career touchdown record lasted sixty-five years.

"You think, 'Oh, he was just running against some old, slow, fat guys,' but I watched film on him and he really was a hell of a player," said Floyd Peters, an NFL

player, scout, or coach for nearly forty years. "He had a beautiful gliding style and also the burst and the speed. He was head and shoulders above the people of his day as far as athleticism, agility, and quickness."

"He was a better runner than Bronko Nagurski, maybe better than Jim Brown," said Steelers president Dan Rooney. "Red Grange changed the game…got the NFL going."

Grange didn't dominate the NFL for very long, but his magnificent college career and his importance in popularizing professional football makes him not only one of the all-time great running backs, but one of the greatest football players of all time.

"In those days, you can't divorce his college career," Giants general manager George Young said. "You can't just say his career was the NFL. It was a combination. He came here in 1925, and that was the big thing that really helped the NFL. At times, he was bigger than the game. He dominated his time. That's the key."

Red Grange became a legend because of the performance he put on in this college game, when he almost single-handedly led Illinois to a 39–14 romp over Michigan in 1924.

FRANCO HARRIS

Oakland's Jimmy Warren waves good-bye to Franco Harris as the great fullback scores after catching a deflected pass on December 23, 1972. Franco's "Immaculate Reception" became the most famous play in NFL history and launched the Steelers' incredible playoff run in the seventies.

For forty years, Art Rooney had owned the Steelers, and never had sports' most beloved man seen them win a playoff game. And now here he was stuck in the stadium elevator, ready to console his losers again, when the "Immaculate Reception" rescued them.

On fourth and 10 with twenty-two seconds left, Terry Bradshaw was about to get leveled when he flung a prayer toward John "Frenchy" Fuqua, who got crunched by "The Assassin," Jack Tatum. The ball bounced off Tatum and was sailing toward the ground and what appeared to be the end of the game. That is, until Franco Harris, who was 15 yards away, plucked the ball off his shoestrings and raced 60 yards for the winning touchdown. Or had he?

Long seconds passed, the officials huddled, and still they signaled nothing. According to the 1972 rules, if the ball last touched Fuqua, the catch didn't count, and the Raiders had won. Crew chief Fred Swearington called upstairs to league officiating supervisor Art McNally, who suspected what the crew suspected: that both Fuqua and Tatum touched the ball. Swearington hung up the phone, ran to the field, and raised both arms.

Three Rivers Stadium roared. The Steelers had won. The Steelers had arrived. They would lose in the next round, but this was to be the start of their dynasty. They would win four Super Bowls in six years, and Franco Harris would be at the heart of it all.

It was the greatest, weirdest, most famous play in NFL history, and neither the Steelers' owner nor their quarterback ever saw it. Mystery still shrouds the play today. The Raiders insist they were cheated. Fuqua remains coy, joking that he won't reveal the truth until he writes a book or is paid millions. The truth, Steelers linebacker Andy Russell confesses, is that Fuqua admitted to him in the locker room that the ball touched him first. However, Russell explained the rule to Fuqua and told him to tell the media the ball had bounced off Tatum.

Harris insists he never knew if the ball hit Fuqua or the ground and that he never got a straight answer from Frenchy. "I honestly don't know." Harris said. "That adds to the mystique of it." But he knows this: when he heard that the artificial turf in Three Rivers was being replaced, he ran to the stadium, found the spot where he caught the ball, and saved that chunk. "Ironically, they were just taking that piece up. I have it. I cannot believe it. I picked the yard line and it was right there."

Just like Franco was always there when the Steelers needed him.

He didn't have Jim Brown's size, O.J. Simpson's speed, or Gale Sayers' moves. He didn't have one particularly monster year, and he didn't leave gracefully, departing for a bad Seattle team in an ugly contract dispute and failing to top Brown's rushing record. Still, when he retired, he had nine Pro Bowl invitations, a record eight 1,000-yard seasons, and twenty-four NFL records. He still ranks fifth in rushing yards (12,130), ninth in combined yards (14,622), and ninth in touchdowns (100).

"People just assumed he was great because everything else was great about the team," ex-teammate Ray Mansfield said. "Maybe he didn't have the biggest year, but you know what about Franco Harris? He didn't give a damn about personal records. He had a total lack of ego when it came to piling up yards. You look at the big

games we played, and Franco always had his best day. You look at the games where we crushed teams and really didn't need him, and those are the games he didn't gain 100 yards."

Indeed, he ran for 1,556 yards and 16 scores in 19 playoff games, including a Super Bowl–record 354 yards and 4 scores. He had 111 yards and 2 touchdowns to beat the Raiders for the 1974 AFC title and a then-record 158 yards as MVP of the Steelers' first Super Bowl win.

"He was just a prince, the most unselfish superstar I ever played with," Bradshaw said. "He was a tailback playing fullback, quick as a cat."

"He was a clutch runner," Russell said. "When you needed 4 yards for the first down, he did it. Franco was a little like Jim Brown in that he could combine power with very elusive halfback qualities. He had a stutter step that would screw people up, but he'd also bull over people."

Harris would tell his blockers to let defenders go whatever way they wanted, and he would find the hole, but to keep blocking, because he might come back their way again.

"We had an off-tackle play called 18 or 19 Straight," Mansfield said. "Sometimes he ran 19 Straight and it wound up looking like 18 Straight, which was the opposite side. He was great. People criticized him for stopping and stuttering, but why? He had such great ability to find the hole and then turn it back on. And Franco was fast! I can't think of how many times he just ran away from defensive backs."

Harris made the Hall of Fame the first year he was eligible and received a champagne toast from two Hall of Fame ex-teammates, Joe Greene and Mel Blount. He was "one of those people who belong automatically," Steelers president Dan Rooney said.

"Franco is the guy who made it happen for the Steelers," Greene said. "Prior to Franco's arrival, we won maybe 6 games. It wasn't a team that had a lot of confidence. When Franco started to run, he uplifted the entire team. We took a quantum leap."

HUGH McELHENNY

In the 1950s, if someone was talking about "The King," the person was usually referring to Elvis Presley. But for football fans, there was also Hugh McElhenny: the king of running backs.

Younger sports fans might not be familiar with McElhenny's name, but if you grew up on the West Coast in the fifties, it is unlikely you could forget it.

"He was from the University of Washington, and we only got the 49ers games back in Washington State, so I watched him through the fifties and then played against him," said Ray Mansfield, who grew up in Seattle watching McElhenny in awe, before his own long career with the awe-inspiring Steelers of the seventies. "He was a classic runner. The King! Get some old 49er highlight films and look at him. Take a look at a guy I thought was the greatest in the open field. You have to see this man run and use his blockers. It was just the most beautiful thing you've ever seen. I loved him as a kid and thought maybe I was prejudiced, but recently I saw a film of great backs and he was included, and then I remembered why I thought he was so great."

Mansfield is not alone in his opinion. The King was inducted into the Pro Football Hall of Fame twenty-five years ago, and when you ask the experts about the best backs they've seen, his name always comes up. Steve Sabol, who has studied all the great backs, says McElhenny, Jim Brown, Gale Sayers, and O.J. Simpson are the best pure runners in NFL history. He says he admires McElhenny's style more than anyone's.

"McElhenny was an incredibly beautiful runner," Sabol said. "He ran with the ball the way little boys do in their wildest dreams. There was a time when he was given an award by the football writers, and the plaque said, 'Wouldn't football be a beautiful game if everybody played it like Hugh McElhenny?'"

You need to see McElhenny run to appreciate his ability because his stats won't wow you. He ran for just 5,281 yards in thirteen seasons, only once gaining more than 700 yards. But he spent his best years sharing the ball with three other Hall of Famers in the 49ers' million-dollar backfield before joining the expansion Vikings in 1961. Still, he led the league in rushing average twice, with a whopping 7.0 in 1952 and 8.0 in 1954. He scored 38 times as a runner, 20 as a receiver (he averaged 12.3 yards on 264 catches), and twice as a punt returner. When he retired in 1964, he had gone to six Pro Bowls and was only the third player with 11,000 combined yards.

"A complete player," said Jack Faulkner, who's spent six decades in pro football and considers McElhenny one of the twenty greatest players—not just backs—he's ever seen.

The King could put on sudden bursts of blinding speed, could fake out half a team, and could change pace and sidestep tacklers.

Colts coach Ted Marchibroda said that McElhenny was "the greatest broken-field runner I've ever seen."

His graceful style emerged after he severed all the tendons in his foot when he was eleven. Doctors said he'd never walk again. Guess he showed them.

"When I was a little kid, my mother would send me to the store at night," McElhenny told NFL Films. "I had to walk down this alley, and at the end of the alley, where the grocery store was, there was a light. The rest of the alley was dark. I used to be scared to go down the alley, so I'd run it. Going through the alley during the day, I'd know where someone might be hiding, so at night, I'd run through there and stay away from the dangerous areas. That's kinda the way I ran the football: with the feeling of fright."

Hugh McElhenny always got the groceries home to his mother, and later in life always scared the daylights out of the opposition.

"Hugh McElhenny was the most colorful runner who's ever played the game, and maybe the best, I'm not positive about that," Y.A. Tittle said. "When he would cross the line of scrimmage, everyone came to their feet because he was capable of scoring every time."

Hugh McElhenny averaged an incredible 8 yards a carry for the 1954 season. He got "only" 6 on this sprint around right end against the Bears on October 31, 1954.

MARION MOTLEY

Jackie Robinson is universally famous for being the first to break the color barrier in major-league baseball in 1947.

But one year before Robinson joined the Brooklyn Dodgers, blacks had integrated pro football; but then, as now, they were little more than footnotes in history. Why? Well, pro football hadn't yet captivated the nation and baseball really was America's pastime. In addition, only a few blacks had played pro football up until the mid-thirties.

The door was opened for good in 1946 by two teams with Cleveland roots. The Cleveland Rams won the 1945 NFL title, then moved to Los Angeles and signed two black stars, Kenny Washington and Woody Strode. At about the same time, Paul Brown's Cleveland franchise in the new All-American Football Conference signed fullback Marion Motley and guard Bill Willis. Washington and Strode played only briefly, but Motley and Willis enjoyed outstanding careers with the Browns in the AAFC and later the NFL, despite enduring the same racial taunts, intimidation, and indignities heaped upon Robinson.

On the field, they encountered brutal tactics and cheap shots. It was the rare pileup in which someone didn't stomp Motley's hand, fling an elbow at his head, or throw an uppercut to his belly. And the white officials condoned the transgressions 99 percent of the time. Motley declines to discuss his career publicly anymore, but Hall of Fame curator Joe Horrigan said that Motley still remembers the name of the first official who finally hollered, "That's enough," and threw a flag.

Off the field, they were treated as second-class citizens. "I remember we went down to play Miami one time in 1946 and they told Paul that the two black guys had to stay at a different hotel," Browns quarterback Otto Graham recalled. "Paul said, 'OK, let's all go.' The whole team was going to go, but then the hotel changed its mind and let us stay. That stuff went on all the time."

Motley was a trailblazer in more ways than one. He was the first ever to catch a screen pass or run a draw play, though both came about more by accident than design. Motley was a six-foot-one-inch, 238-pound bull of a runner, but more important, he made Brown's revolutionary passing game work with his blocking for Graham. "Motley would pick up a blitz," said Weeb Ewbank, ex–Browns assistant and later the Super Bowl Jets coach, "and when he did, it was too bad for the fellow blitzing. He'd hit him so hard that he'd knock him right back to the line."

But one time the pass rushers got to Graham and he handed the ball to Motley in desperation. The defense had overrun Motley, and he blasted through the big gap on the right side for a big gain, giving football the draw play. Another time, a harried Graham flipped a little pass to Motley, and thus was born the screen pass and one of the most terrifying sights in sports: a bull moose on the loose.

"I will never forget a game in 1952 in Cleveland when I had my first chance to tackle Marion Motley," said Hall of Famer Dick "Night Train" Lane. "He looked like a big tank rolling down on me. But you've got to take him on. I hit him with my head in my knees, and he came down. I saw a few stars, but I felt good because I tackled Marion Motley."

Motley wore No. 76 (running backs usually wear lower numbers), and that was appropriate, because he was "really a tackle with the ball under his arm, running over people," recalled Floyd Peters, a former Brown and longtime NFL coach. "And he was fast, too."

Motley is not nearly as famous as the Browns fullback who followed him, Jim Brown, but the experts know how good he was. He was one of seven running backs on the NFL's seventy-fifth anniversary all-time All-Pro team, joining Brown, Walter Payton, O.J. Simpson, Gale Sayers, Steve Van Buren, and Bronko Nagurski, and beating out such stars as Jim Thorpe, Red

Grange, Hugh McElhenny, Tony Dorsett, Franco Harris, Eric Dickerson, Emmitt Smith, and Barry Sanders. Motley, who also played strongside linebacker his first two years, was the first black inducted into the Hall of Fame and made the all-time All-Two-Way Team, too.

"He could do everything," said Bucko Kilroy.

Motley was twenty-six when he joined the Browns after leaving the navy. His best years came in the AAFC, which he led with 3,024 yards, 31 touchdowns, and a 6.2-yard average. In the Browns' first season in the league, he led the NFL in rushing. He averaged 5.8 yards a carry that year and 5.7 for his nine-year pro career, which, if the NFL counted AAFC statistics,

would better Brown's record by half a yard. He still holds the NFL record for highest average in a single game, with 188 yards, 17.1 per crack, versus the 1950 Steelers.

Motley might have set all kinds of records if he had run more often, but the Browns were filled with stars. They played in an incredible 10 straight championship games, winning all four AAFC titles and three of six NFL titles. Brown built their attack around the passing of Graham and the blocking of Motley, who may be the best blocking back of all time.

"[He was] the most unselfish player I ever coached," Brown said.

Marion Motley (76), shown here bulling 11 yards for a first down versus the New York Giants in 1950, was one of the toughest all-around players in football history. Motley was a pioneer as one of the first black players in the modern game.

57

BRONKO NAGURSKI

You don't have to see the faded photos of the big, thick guy in the leather helmet and black high-tops, don't have to see the grainy film of him busting through tacklers as if they were turnstiles. Just the name conjures up an image.

Bronko Nagurski. Has there ever been a better name for a football player? Has there ever been a better all-around football player?

The funny thing is, Bronko's nickname initially had nothing to do with football; his first teacher simply botched Bronislau, the name given to him by his Ukrainian immigrant parents. Later, Bronko's nickname had everything to do with football. He was the ultimate bruising fullback that no man could tackle. Now, more than fifty years after he played, he remains the standard by which all rugged runners are measured.

Still, sometimes it's hard to tell man from myth. Like another legend from his region, Paul Bunyan, Bronko inspired stories that might be apocryphal but sure are colorful. His coach at the University of Minnesota, Clarence "Doc" Spears, claimed to recruit him after seeing him plowing a field without a horse. Doc said he asked for directions and Bronko lifted the plow to his shoulders and pointed its tip toward the proper path.

They say Bronko crashed through the end zone so powerfully once that he knocked over a mounted policeman, horse and all. They say he once missed a tackle, slammed into a Model T, and sheared off the fender. They also say he scored against the Redskins when he knocked two linebackers in opposite directions, stomped over a defensive back, crushed a safety, and caromed off the goalposts and into Wrigley Field's brick wall, putting a crack in it. "That last guy hit me awfully hard," he supposedly said when he ran back to the huddle.

But this is true: Bronko won All-American recognition three straight seasons, in the third becoming the only player in history ever honored as an All-American at two different positions in a single season: defensive tackle and fullback.

Minnesota's famed Iron Man rose to even greater heights as a line-crashing runner, blocker, defensive lineman, and linebacker for the Chicago Bears. He was six feet two inches and 235 pounds, which was big for a lineman in the thirties, let alone a back. He was so strong that they used to say Bronko was the only man who could run interference for himself.

"I was a straight downfield runner," Bronko said. "I wouldn't, or rather couldn't, dodge anybody. If somebody got in my way, I ran through them."

Though he was just a boy when Nagurski played, Dan Rooney will never forget the way Nagurski ran "through our whole team."

"I was just a kid, but I remember sitting with my mother in the box and he ran through the team three times," said Rooney, who now runs the Pittsburgh club that his father founded in 1933. "He ran over

people; he wouldn't be tackled. He didn't play running back all the time, though. He dominated on defense, too."

Bronko was such a devastating blocker that he was credited as the key to Beattie Feathers' running for 1,004 yards in 1934, the only 1,000-yard performance in NFL history until 1947. He threw for the only touchdown (to Red Grange) of the title game in 1932, the first of his three NFL titles. And he was such a good defender that he was voted All-Pro six of his nine years, was a charter member of the Hall of Fame, and made the NFL's seventy-fifth anniversary all-time All-Pro team in 1994.

"He was as good a linebacker as an offensive back," said Bucko Kilroy, who played against an older Nagurski in 1943. "He was an exceptionally hard guy to bring down."

Bronko was voted the third-best player of the half-century, trailing only Jim Thorpe and Grange. But not everyone agreed. Grantland Rice wrote, "Eleven Bronko Nagurskis could beat eleven Red Granges or eleven Jim Thorpes."

Or eleven pro wrestlers. The Hulk Hogan of his time, he juggled both sports for a while, playing in 5 Bears games and wrestling in eight cities in one amazing three-week span in 1937. But when Halas refused to pay him six thousand dollars in 1938, Bronko left football for wrestling, uttering one of the most memorable lines in NFL history: "Halas tossed nickels around like they were manhole covers."

Bronko returned for one last hurrah in 1943, when the Bears were shorthanded during the war. At age thirty-five, he was not as quick as he once was and played mostly tackle, but still crashed through bodies for a touchdown in the NFL title game.

Bronko continued wrestling until he was fifty-two, and he lived to the age of eighty-one.

Visiters to the Hall of Fame in Canton, Ohio still gape at his championship ring—size 19½, so big that you can pass a regular-sized ring through it with ease—proving that even in death, Bronko remains larger than life.

Bucking the Brooklyn Dodgers' defense as he helps the Bears claw their way to victory at Ebbets Field, Bronko Nagurski was a charter member of the Pro Football Hall of Fame, and was so tough that he had a second pro career in wrestling. "People told me I could get into wrestling and make millions," he said. "I did it for about twelve, thirteen, fourteen years. It was tough work, and I didn't make millions."

WALTER PAYTON

Bill Tobin was a pretty fair running back for Missouri many years ago. More importantly, though, he helped the Bears make Walter Payton the fourth choice in the 1975 draft. "The total package is what we draft for, and he was the total package. He had great anticipation and great eyes and great strength and sensational durability—a huge, huge competitor. He was a solid person, a leader. He was outstanding at breaking tackles. For his size, he's the strongest human I've been around.

"When you put it all together—hands, intelligence, blocking—Walter Payton is the best of all time. Jim Brown was not a blocker. When they threw the ball, he was taking the play off. When they handed the ball to someone else, he took the play off. That wasn't true with Walter Payton."

Ask Payton to name his favorite play, and he mentions not a run or catch but a block. His backfield coach, Johnny Roland, said he "doesn't block people, he buries them." His head coach, Mike Ditka, said he once took on two Bengals blitzers "and would have liked to have killed them." His late general manager, Jim Finks, said he was the NFL's finest back and blocker. "He flattens linebackers, he knocks down ends, he attacks nose guards. And the irony is that he's competing against a one-dimensional player. When Brown wasn't carrying the ball, he rested."

Let Ditka expound: "It's possible nobody ever cut like Sayers. And maybe nobody ever ran like Brown or slashed like O.J. But without a doubt, Walter is the most complete football player I've ever seen. He may not do some things as well as someone else has done, but everything he does, [he does] better than anyone else ever has. When God said He would make a halfback or a fullback, He might have said Gale Sayers or He might have said Jim Brown. But when He said that He would make the best football player who ever lived, He probably said two men: Jim Thorpe and Walter Payton."

Payton never cared for comparisons, saying it was like "trying to draw the wind. You know it's there, but there isn't any way you can accurately describe it." No, he preferred to be remembered like "Charlie Hustle," Pete Rose: "not as the best runner, but as a guy who gave all he had."

Payton's off-season workouts were the stuff of legend. He'd sprint a steep, sandy hill for an hour straight, exhausting himself so thoroughly that he'd collapse, unable to move for forty-five minutes. When even the best-conditioned athletes tried to match him, he'd leave them heaving.

In college, Payton set an NCAA scoring record, averaged more than 6 yards a carry, punted, kicked field goals and extra points, returned kicks, and completed 14 of 19 passes, 4 of them for touchdowns.

In the pros, Payton accumulated 16,726 yards, smashing Jim Brown's rushing record by 4,414 yards, which is comparable to Hank Aaron hitting 257 more homers than Babe Ruth. His 21,803 combined yards surpassed Brown's mark by 6,344. And while it's true that he played four years and 72 games more than Brown, he broke the rushing record in 120 games, just 2 more than Brown played, and would have done it in nine years, just as Brown had, if he hadn't lost 7 games to the 1982 strike. That year, plus his first and last, were the only ones he didn't run for at least 1,200 yards. One should also take into consideration that Brown played on a better team; Cleveland was 79-34-1 in his nine years, and Chicago was 61–70 in Payton's first nine.

Payton missed only 1 game in all of his thirteen seasons, because of a coach's decision. He was the league MVP twice, a Pro Bowler nine times, ran for 1,000 yards in 10 seasons, and had 77 100-yard games. He ran for 110 touchdowns, which was another of his eight NFL and twenty-six Chicago record marks. Payton also caught 491 passes, which was a running-back record until 1991.

Those who remember Walter Payton purely for his work ethic slight his athleticism. Ted Marchibroda, who has played or coached in the NFL for four decades, calls Walter Payton "the greatest all-around athlete I've seen." He beat seven-foot-two-inch Artis Gilmore one-on-one in basketball. He bench-pressed 390 pounds and leg-pressed 700. He walked the width of a football field on his hands. He could rip a live tree that was a foot in circumference out of the ground with his bare hands. He once leapfrogged over the head of a six-foot-four assistant coach, booted a kickoff through the uprights with a running back's shoe, and matched one of the quarterbacks blister for blister in a game of burn-out, catching the ball at short distance.

"He's not in Jim Brown's category or even Gale Sayers' as a pure runner," NFL Films president Steve Sabol said. "But certainly the greatest running back, when you look at the whole position, was Walter Payton. More than a runner, Walter Payton was a football player. I saw him lift blitzing linebackers off their feet. I saw him punt 60 yards in practice. He once led the league in kick returns. He's the Bears' all-time leading receiver. And when he threw passes, he completed eight of them for touchdowns. He even played quarterback for 1 game in 1984.

"He got his name 'Sweetness' for sweet moves, but I think they got it all wrong. He could fake and juke with the best of them, but what Payton really liked to do was run over people. I think 'Toughness' would have been a better name for Payton.

"I remember the day in 1977 in Soldier Field against the Vikings when he broke the [single-game] record. I was a cameraman that day, and I overheard the team doctor say that he didn't think Walter Payton was gonna start because he had the flu. Payton started and then he carried 40 times for 275 yards, farther than anyone ever. I don't know if that story's ever been told, but I was there. I heard the doctor. To turn around and have the greatest day a runner ever had, that says something about the guy."

BARRY SANDERS

Barry Sanders' moves seem to come from divine inspiration at times.

"God only put one pair of feet like that on a human being," Green Bay defensive coordinator Fritz Shurmur said.

"When God created Barry Sanders, even He didn't know what He made," Fox television network's Matt Millen said.

And Detroit coach Wayne Fontes said, "The guy upstairs, He's got a plan. He had a plan to make Einstein. He made Barry the way he is."

He is bigger than life. Want proof? Check out his mural on the side of the Cadillac Towers in downtown Detroit. It's fifteen stories high.

Sanders has more moves than a knuckleball in a hurricane and more twists and turns than a pretzel factory. "Barry's a work of art," said Lions teammate Herman Moore, himself a Pro Bowl receiver. "It just seems so natural, the moves he does. If I tried to do it, I'd pop a knee."

Only Eric Dickerson, O.J. Simpson, and Earl Campbell ever ran for more yards in one season than Sanders did in 1994, and of those, only O.J. averaged more yards per carry. Only Sanders has run for 200 yards in a single half of a game. Sanders and Dickerson are the only two players to run for 1,000 yards in six of their first seven seasons, but Sanders has done something Dickerson never did: he touched the ball 803 consecutive times without losing it.

There are only nine men who have ever run for more yards than Sanders, and if he maintains his seven-year pace of 1,453 yards a year, he will surpass Walter Payton as the league's number one runner when he's thirty-two, in the year 2000.

Payton has already conceded. "He's better than I was," Payton said when Sanders was just a rookie. "I was never that good."

Sanders averages 4.9 yards a carry, half a yard better than Payton and Dickerson, better than everyone in the top twenty save Jim Brown. That's probably the best measure of a back's ability and elusiveness. Considering that Sanders has never played with a great line or great team, that fact is even more impressive. Emmitt Smith might have a lion's heart, but there's only one Lion King. Even Dallas coach Barry Switzer admits Sanders is "the most dangerous back in the league" today—and maybe ever.

"He's the best runner that's ever touched the football," Fontes said. "If anybody thinks he isn't, then they're not watching football."

Gale Sayers said that Sanders is the only back today who reminds him of himself. Steve Sabol said, "You could put him in a phone booth with someone else and it'd be ten minutes before the other guy could touch him." Green Bay coach Mike Holmgren said that Sanders is "quicker than any man I've ever seen." Detroit assistant head coach Dave Levy, who coached O.J., said that Sanders has the best balance he's ever seen. Ex–Vikings coach Jerry Burns says that Sanders has Earl Campbell's leg strength and is so slippery, that he must wear silicone spray on his jersey. The officials checked; he doesn't. Seattle safety Eugene Robinson said that Sanders combines Barry Foster's power and Smith's elusiveness. "Oh boy, can he make you miss."

Just ask Patriot safety Harlon Barnett. Sanders turned him around on one play. Or ask the Tampa Bay Buccaneers. One of their defensive men yanked off his shoe 7 yards downfield, but none could tackle him until 78 yards later.

Sanders burst into the nation's consciousness in 1988. After being Thurman Thomas' backup for two years at Oklahoma State, he set thirteen NCAA records with 2,628 rushing yards and 39 touchdowns.

Barry Sanders often leaves defenders grasping for air, as he does here to Pro Bowl linebacker Shane Conlan of the Rams. As his television commercial suggests, he's the Cadillac of running backs. When he turned a simple draw play into a 37-yard thing of beauty on October 29, 1995, he surpassed Earl Campbell as the tenth leading rusher in NFL history. That gave him 9,510 yards in exactly six and a half seasons. All-time leader Walter Payton had 16,726 in thirteen years.

Still, when he chose to turn pro early, the NFL scouts had two worries. First, the Heisman Trophy winner was only five feet eight inches tall. Second, the Dallas Cowboys and Green Bay Packers had committed the first two picks to Troy Aikman and Tony Mandarich, and with the third pick, Detroit was considering Barry Sanders, Deion Sanders, and Tim Worley. However, when a bunch of clubs finally trekked out to Stillwater, Oklahoma to watch Sanders work out, the debate soon ended.

He covered 40 yards in 4.27 seconds; covered 40, 41, and 42 inches in his vertical jumps; and made 11 feet from a standing broad jump.

Fontes lit a cigar like a proud new papa, unable to conceal his grin. "My running back won't be doing anything else today," he told the other scouts. "Thank you for coming."

"Everybody thought I was kidding," Fontes later recalled. "I wasn't."

Still, the Lions didn't sign Sanders until just two days before the opener. He had time to learn just four plays, only one well. No practice? No matter. On his first carry he ran for 18 yards and on his fourth carry he scored a touchdown. On his fifth carry he gained 26 yards, and by the end of the quarter—after 9 carries—he had gained 71 yards.

In Sanders' next game, six-foot-four-inch, 235-pound All-Pro Carl Banks nailed him dead-on, but Sanders broke the tackle. On the following Sunday, Sanders had his first 100-yard game by halftime, versus the Bears. Three games into Sanders' pro career, Mike Ditka surrendered. Ditka had coached or played with Payton, Sayers, and Tony Dorsett. "Barry Sanders," he said, "is as fine a running back as I've ever seen."

GALE SAYERS

Forget the numbers, the records, the superlatives. They cannot do Gale Sayers justice.

To see him run is to see "magic in motion," George Halas said. "If you wish to see perfection, you had best get hold of a film of Gale Sayers."

It is good advice. Sayers made moves that the eyes cannot believe. "I thought I saw him become amoeba-like, a paramecium that split into two, and the defensive people went at the wrong one," comedian Bill Cosby told NFL Films.

Hall of Famer Herb Adderley says, "He's the only guy who could be running, stop on a dime, tell you where to pick up the change, and not even break stride."

Sayers scored a record-tying 6 touchdowns against the 49ers in 1965, and he could have broken the NFL standard if Halas, the Bears' coach and owner, hadn't taken him out near the goal line or if he hadn't slipped in the thick midfield mud after returning a punt for 32 yards. As it was, Halas, part of pro football from 1919 until the day he died in 1983, called it "the greatest football exhibition I have ever seen." Vince Lombardi called Sayers' 205 yards in the Green Bay mud during the Packers' dynastic heyday the finest performance he'd ever seen.

Sayers scored a then-record 22 touchdowns and amassed 2,272 combined yards despite playing just 12 full games in his sensational 1965 rookie year. The next year, he led the league in rushing (1,231 yards, 5.4 average) and kick returns (2 TDs, 31.2 average). In 1968, he averaged an astonishing 26.7 yards per punt return and 37.7 per kick return, bringing back 4 of 19 returns for scores until tearing up his knee. However, Sayers became the first back to run for 1,000 yards the first season after major knee surgery, in 1969 (he gave his Most Courageous Player award to his dying running mate, Brian Piccolo). But another knee injury in 1970 reduced him to just 4 games over the next two years and forced him to retire, the owner of nine NFL and sixteen Chicago rushing records.

Despite playing just 68 games in seven years, Sayers was elected to the Hall of Fame on the first ballot. At thirty-four years of age, he was the youngest ever. He was voted to both the NFL's fiftieth and seventy-fifth anniversary all-time All-Pro teams, and most longtime pros call him the most exciting, elusive runner ever.

"My game was quickness. I had a great first two or three steps," Sayers said. "There was no excitement for me to go 65 yards for a touchdown or 90 or 103 yards on a kick return. Once you're in the open, anyone can run. That's not exciting. The excitement for me was the first 10 or 20 yards. What did you do to get in the open? Did you have to fake out one person? Did you have to stiff-arm somebody? Did you have to spin around somebody else? Did you have to run by somebody? That was the excitement.

Imagine if today's medical technology had been available then.

"I probably would have played another two, three, four years," Sayers said. "Every surgery I had, I was in a cast from hip to toe for ten weeks. Today, you don't even have a cast on. They do arthroscopic surgery and the next day you're in the swimming pool kicking."

Imagine if he had played on artificial turf.

"I played on mud and grass and dirt. I didn't play on Astroturf. I was quick, and turf makes you quicker."

Imagine if he'd played on a great team. Even with him, the Bears had just two winning seasons.

"Man alive, I would have liked to have seen what records he would have set," Super Bowl Steeler Ray Mansfield said.

No matter. His moves were more memorable than any record could be.

Gale Sayers shakes off Kermit Alexander (39) and runs 21 yards for one of his incredible 6 scores versus San Francisco on December 12, 1965. Despite playing just five full seasons, he retired with nine NFL and sixteen Chicago records.

O.J. SIMPSON

President of the treasure trove that is NFL Films, Steve Sabol has watched as much football film as any man alive, and still cannot compare Orenthal James Simpson to any other back. O.J. reminds him not of mere mortals, but of mythical men and Greek gods.

"I compare him to a figure in Greek mythology, Antaeus," Sabol said. "He became stronger every time he bounced off the ground. When I think of O.J., I think of Antaeus. The more O.J. carried and got hit, the better he got. Lou Saban used to call him a sooner-or-later back, because sooner or later, no matter how hard you made it for him, O.J. would beat you."

Until Saban became their coach, the Bills and O.J. didn't beat anybody. The two-time All-American never topped even 750 yards or 4 victories his first three pro seasons. Buffalo fans moaned that he was another Heisman flop, and O.J. contemplated quitting. One coach tried to make him a wide receiver. Another tried to make him a power back, which former opponent Murray Warmath said was like "trying to put plumber's tools in the hands of a violinist." Then Saban arrived and turned the Juice loose.

"I couldn't believe how little O.J. had been used," Saban said. "Here we had someone with the talents to be the greatest running back ever. And I, for one, intended to use those talents."

O.J. won the 1972 rushing title with 1,251 yards, but that was just the warm-up act to 1973, when he set then–NFL records for single-season and single-game yards, and 100-yard and 200-yard games in a season. Before O.J., 1,000-yard seasons and 100-yard games were the mark of excellence. He'd get 1,000 by October and 100 by halftime. Consider the final game of 1973, when he needed 61 yards to crack Jim Brown's "unbreakable" record and 197 for the "unreachable" 2,000-yard barrier. He had to do it on hell frozen over, all snow and ice and mud, but O.J. had 108 yards by halftime. When he plowed through the snow for 200 yards and the record, his teammates lifted him onto their shoulders and, for once, carried him.

Eric Dickerson would break O.J.'s records for single-season yards and 100-yard games, but he would need 2 more games and 47 more carries; Dickerson had but 1,781 yards and a 5.4-yard average through 14 games. O.J. had 2,003 yards and a scintillating 6.0-yard average.

In the greatest five-year stretch of any running back ever, O.J. averaged 110 yards per game and was voted Player of the Year three times. His six 200-yard games are still a record today, and his 273- and 250-yard games still trail only Walter Payton's 275. He retired tailing only Brown in career total yards. Now six men have gained more, but of them, only Brown averaged more yards per carry.

We can only imagine the records Simpson could have set if he hadn't been misused his first three seasons, if he hadn't suffered through knee problems his final two seasons, and if he hadn't played on Bills teams that went just 43-81-2 during his nine years and made the playoffs just once.

He was a regal 212-pounder who ran the hundred in 9.4 seconds, a big, beautiful back who could sweep around the end yet slash inside. He was so graceful, so fluid and fast, that he made everyone else appear to go in slow motion. Those who watched him were filled with wonder, and most rate him just behind Brown as the greatest runner ever, though others put Payton and Sayers in his class.

Ray Mansfield, who won two Super Bowls with the Steelers, remembers seeing his personal top-two backs together in Miami.

"Jimmy Brown was sitting in one of those big fan-backed straw chairs, and O.J. was sitting on the arm of it," he said. "I said to my partner, 'Look, the king and the crown prince.' I went over and shook hands and said, 'I know you don't know who I am, but I played against both of you,' and O.J. looked at my Super Bowl ring and said, 'Hey, buddy, when you wear one of those, you don't have to apologize to anybody.' "

O.J. never did win a title, perhaps the only thing missing from his career. Antaeus was mortal, after all.

With his incredible speed and rapid instincts, O.J. Simpson was a master at finding holes in a defense. Here, he looks to charge between two Tampa Bay Bucaneer defenders.

EMMITT SMITH

RIGHT: **In the defining game of his career, Emmitt Smith displayed his courage and his talent, gaining 229 yards rushing and receiving to spark the Cowboys to the1993 NFC East title.**

OPPOSITE: **In another typical performance, Smith runs for 171 yards and a touchdown as Dallas opens the 1994 season by routing a good Steelers team in Pittsburgh.**

The commercial opens with Emmitt Smith about to be corralled by two Colts. They are right in his face, poised to pounce. They can't miss him, can they?

Yes, they can.

In an instant, Emmitt goes from full speed to sudden stop to cougarlike crouch to 180-degree spin. And then he is gone.

Smith has more moves than just about any back today, but he's not Barry Sanders. Smith has decent size and speed, but he's not nearly as big as Jim Brown or Franco Harris, and not nearly as fast as O.J. Simpson or Eric Dickerson. If he resembles any great back, it's Walter Payton, the all-time rushing champion he seeks to surpass.

Payton was five feet eleven inches and 202 pounds, and ran the forty in 4.55 to 4.6 seconds.

Smith is five feet nine inches and 209 pounds, and runs the forty in 4.55 to 4.6 seconds.

Both have pinball moves and sure hands, exceptional balance and vision, tackle-breaking thighs, plowhorse durability, and a championship heart.

Who can forget Smith's performance in the 1993 regular-season finale? Smith separated his right shoulder late in the second quarter, but with the division title and rushing title at stake, he refused to leave. His right arm dangling uselessly and his face grimacing noticeably, Smith had to be helped by his teammates off the ground and back to the huddle after every play. Undeterred, Smith established a Dallas record for rushing-receiving attempts that day. He ran 32 times for 168 yards and caught 10 passes for another 61 yards, lifting the Cowboys to a 16–13 overtime victory. He scored the team's only touchdown and even lowered his lame shoulder to block a blitzing linebacker. On 9 of the 12 plays of Dallas' winning drive, Smith carried the ball for 41 of the 52 yards.

"You know, a lot of people talk about what a great and courageous performance that was," Giants coach Dan Reeves told Smith after the season. "But it made me want to throw up."

It would have made a lesser man give up the next 2 playoff games, but Smith, in obvious pain, still managed 148 yards. And then in the Super Bowl, with Troy Aikman still suffering the aftereffects of a severe concussion and the Cowboys trailing 13–6 at halftime, Smith demanded, "Get me the ball."

Dallas did. After tying the game on a fumble return, the Cowboys gave Smith the ball 7 of 8 plays, in a go-ahead drive capped by his 15-yard score. Smith, who'd run for 100 yards in all 3 postseason games when the Cowboys won Super Bowl XXVII, finished the game with 132 yards, 2 touchdowns, and the MVP trophy for Super Bowl XXVIII.

Only once in five years has Smith missed a start because of injuries. And not once did he fumble in 1994. He's the only player to win the rushing title and Super Bowl in the same season, and he did it twice in a row. Smith is the only player to win the rushing title, regular season MVP, and Super Bowl MVP in the same season, and he is the only player to run for 1,400 yards in five consecutive seasons. Smith joined Jim Brown, Earl Campbell, and Steve Van Buren as the only backs to win three straight rushing titles.

Smith is the only indispensable Cowboy. "It's been proven," Reggie White said. "They've won without Troy. They never win without Emmitt." Because as good as the Cowboys are, they were 1–15 before he arrived and winless in the 3 starts he's missed since. "We gotta have him," then–Dallas center Mark Stepnoski said in 1994. "He's the best back in the league."

He's a winner. He's 63–26 as a starter and 33–3 when he runs for 100 yards.

He's a receiver. He's averaged nearly 50 catches a year.

He's a scorer. If a pulled hamstring didn't cost him 1½ games in '94, he might have broken the NFL touchdown record. As it was, only John Riggins ever ran for more, and only Riggins, Simpson, and Jerry Rice ever had more total TDs. With 25 in 1995 and 71 from 1990 to 1994, Smith has a real shot at Payton's record for rushing TDs (110).

Even though Smith set fifty-eight school records at Florida University, such lemons as Blair Thomas, Keith McCants, Andre Ware, Chris Singleton, Ray Agnew, Percy Snow, and James Williams were chosen before him in 1990. The Cowboys finally made him the seventeenth pick and Smith quickly proved to be the draft's best player.

He wants to be history's best back. "I'm playing for something else now," Smith said. "I'm playing for Canton." And for Payton's all-time rushing record of 16,726 yards. "I need to average some ridiculous amount of yardage." Not too ridiculous; if Smith were to maintain his 1,437-yard pace, he'd surpass Sweetness in 2001, just after his thirty-second birthday. If he matches Payton's thirteen seasons, he'd have to average 1,110 yards from 1996 through 2002.

"It's way too soon to think about Payton, but I can't help it," he said. "It's there in the back of my mind. I'm a stubborn person, bullheaded, and if I set my mind to something, I can get it done."

THURMAN THOMAS

Sometimes when Thurman Thomas wants an instant adrenaline surge, he watches a videotape of Draft Day 1988.

It is no human highlight film; it is a chronicle of his humiliation. His heroic comeback from knee surgery, his sensational senior season, his scintillating bowl games, and his scouting workouts all indicated that he should be one of the top ten or twenty choices. But as ESPN's cameras filmed him in his home, he was ignored until the fortieth choice, and his despair and anguish and embarrassment were evident not only to his friends and family, but to all of pro football and millions of television viewers.

It is the day the geniuses slighted Thurman Thomas, and it is a day they will long rue because he has not only proved them wrong, but he has proved them fools. Even as he blossomed into the best all-around back of the nineties, he still watched that tape for inspiration.

"All the time," he said, triumphantly. "All the time."

"Look at all the people who passed him over," said Jack Faulkner of the Rams, who passed him over for Gaston Green. "It can be a great motivator."

"He's quite a self-motivator anyway," backfield coach Elijah Pitts said. "But he had a little something to prove: that everybody was wrong."

Barry Sanders is a better pure runner. Emmitt Smith is a better scorer. Marshall Faulk is quicker. Ronnie Harmon might catch better. A few halfbacks might block better. But Thomas led the NFL in combined rushing-receiving yards four years in a row, eclipsing the record held by the immortal Jim Brown; he carried the Bills to an unprecedented four consecutive Super Bowls, tying a record with scores in all four; he matched Eric Dickerson's NFL record of seven straight 1,000-yard seasons in 1995; and he enters the 1996 season averaging 1,216 rushing yards and 1,669 combined yards. If he maintains that pace for another two years, the Thurmanator will rank fifth in career rushing and second in combined yards, and will be only thirty-one years old.

"He's the best I've been around at all phases of the game," said Pitts, who has played with or coached Hall of Famers Jim Taylor, Paul Hornung, Gale Sayers, and Earl Campbell.

O.J. Simpson calls Thomas "the most complete back in the game. He's an unusual combination of shifty and powerful. He's not quite as elusive as Barry Sanders, but they remind you of each other. Plus, he's a competitor. Most jitterbugs will take the day off when they're not having a good day. The harder Thurman is hit, the harder he comes back."

He hits back, too, though only five foot ten inches and 198 pounds. Bills center Kent Hull said he's not only willing to block blitzers: "He's stoning them, too."

"The total package, it's hard to get a better back," Bills general manager John Butler said. "If you were asking me if I would trade Thurman Thomas for anyone in the NFL, it would be absolutely no. Wouldn't even think of it."

"He is," former Dolphins coach Don Shula said, "just one complete package."

Thomas ran for 1,650 yards as an Oklahoma State sophomore before damaging his knee in a summer pick-up basketball game. He still ran for 741 yards that year. Then, after a second arthroscopic knee surgery, he ran for 1,613 yards and 18 touchdowns. He never missed a game because of the injury. He ran for 157 yards and 4 scores in the Sun Bowl. He was the Senior Bowl's finest player. He kept Sanders on OSU's bench.

Anyone could see that this guy was magnificent. But the scouts, who are paid to see, were scared by Thomas' knee brace, and some team doctors were afraid that his ligament was loose and might give way.

So much for that worry. The 1992 NFL MVP has touched the ball 2,656 times and missed only 5 of 128 games.

"A lot of people were worried about his long-range durability," Steelers boss Tom Donahoe said. "Some teams said he was fine and some red-flagged him. It happens all the time: medical rejects play ten years and guys who didn't have a nick in college can't play a healthy season in the NFL." (Best example: Anthony Munoz, maybe the best lineman ever, was labeled a medical reject by fourteen team doctors, including the one who approved Thomas for the Bills.)

Buffalo rated Thomas as the draft's seventeenth-best player, but lacked a number one pick and figured they would settle for Tony Jeffery or Jamie Morris. But other teams' fear made Thomas the fortieth player and eighth back drafted, behind Green, John Stephens, Lorenzo White, Brad Muster, "Ironhead" Heyward, Ickey Woods, and Jeffery.

"You can't look back. You'll drive yourself crazy," Donahoe explained. "It's like calling plays. They're a lot easier to call on Monday morning than on Sunday afternoon."

Unless you have Thurman Thomas. Then you just call his name.

Thurman Thomas seized two more of the immortal O.J. Simpson's Buffalo records in 1995. He tied O.J.'s Bills record with his forty-first 100-yard game, 133 against the Jets in October, and broke Simpson's career TD mark with his seventy-first against the Patriots in November.

JIM THORPE

Before he became the Allies' supreme commander, Europe's savior, and America's president, Dwight D. Eisenhower was an Army halfback watching Jim Thorpe and tiny underdog Carlisle School trample America's finest.

Angry and embarrassed, Ike vowed to knock Thorpe out of the game. He plowed into Thorpe's shoulders while another cadet crunched into his knees. Thorpe lay there, not moving a muscle, for one or two minutes, so long that West Point thought that he'd have to be carried off on a stretcher.

Ike was certain that Thorpe wouldn't gain another yard all day.

Good thing Ike and Army were more certain against Hitler and his Nazis.

The next play, Thorpe ran for 10 yards. The next kickoff, Thorpe ran all the way, only to have the touchdown called back by an offside penalty. So Army kicked off again, only to have Thorpe score again.

"I guess that was the longest run for a touchdown I ever made," Thorpe later recalled. "Ninety and 95 make 185 yards."

Thus Jim Thorpe and ten nobodies made for a 27–6 victory against a 1912 powerhouse blessed with one future president and four All-Americans. Thorpe played every second of the sixty minutes. Ike limped off the field with a twisted knee that 1 game later forced him to learn another kind of blitzkrieg.

You might say it worked out: Ike led America to victory and prosperity, and Jim Thorpe led America to Olympic glory and the discovery of a passion for pro football.

In polls of writers and broadcasters held in 1950, Thorpe was voted the greatest athlete and the greatest football player of the first half of the century. For greatest athlete, Thorpe received 292 votes, Babe Ruth 86, Jack Dempsey 19, Ty Cobb 11, and Joe Louis 5. For greatest football player, Thorpe had 170, Red Grange 138, and Bronko Nagurski 38.

Thorpe was also named to the NFL's fiftieth-anniversary all-time All-Pro team. He was inducted into three Halls of Fame—college football, professional football, and track and field—and played professional baseball. He batted .327 in the last of his six major league seasons. And as if that weren't enough, Thorpe

also excelled in boxing, lacrosse, basketball, hockey, archery, canoeing, handball, swimming, ice skating, and gymnastics.

James Francis Thorpe was one-eighth Irish, one-eighth Dutch, one-eighth Welsh, five-eighths Indian, and all legend.

Thorpe was the subject of a book and a movie, and even had a town in Pennsylvania named after him. Born in 1888, one hundred years after his great-grandfather Black Hawk had been named chief of the Sac and Fox Indians, he was originally named Wa-Tho-Huck, which means "bright path."

The first time he touched the ball for Carlisle's famous coach, Pop Warner, he lost 5 yards and got reprimanded, which was just what he needed. Thorpe was such a natural, he played hard only when challenged. "Give it to me again," he snarled. "They won't touch me." No one was within 20 yards of him when he crossed the goal line 75 yards later.

A third-team All-American back in 1908, he spent two years playing semipro baseball for sixty dollars a month before returning to Carlisle to make two consecutive first-team All-American teams. In an age when whole teams were lucky to average 10 points a game, Thorpe scored 25 touchdowns and 198 points in 1912.

After two more years in baseball, Thorpe began playing both pro sports simultaneously in 1915 as the Canton Bulldogs' player-coach. When Knute Rockne snuffed several of his favored end runs—Thorpe loved to show off his world-class speed—Thorpe told him to stop, that the fans had come to see him run. "Go ahead and run—if you can," Rockne replied. The next play, Thorpe sent Rockne careening into the Massillon bench and ran 60 yards to score. As a blocker, the 185-pounder knocked 240-pound Steve Owen off his feet and onto his skull. As a defensive back, he could bury runners or dismay quarterbacks with long interception returns. And as a kicker, he could drop-kick field goals from midfield.

When the league that would become the NFL was organized in 1920, Thorpe became its first president and moved from team to team to help balance the com-

petition and box-office draw. He played for Canton, Cleveland, Oorang, Rock Island, New York, Saint Petersburg, Portsmouth, Hammond, and Chicago before retiring at age forty-one in 1929.

Yet Thorpe's greatest feats came in the 1912 Olympics, where he won four of the five events in the pentathlon, including the 200-meter hurdles in a record that stood for thirty-six years. He won four more events in the decathlon and finished nearly 700 points ahead of the runner-up.

King Gustav of Sweden handed Thorpe a bronze bust cast in the monarch's likeness, a silver Viking ship studded with jewels, a laurel wreath, and this compliment: "Sir, you are the greatest athlete in the world." Thorpe returned to parades in New York, Philadelphia, Boston, and Carlisle.

But when the Amateur Athletic Union (AAU) discovered he'd been paid to play baseball—even though the money was minimal and it was a different sport—his name was erased from the Olympic record books, and his awards, worth fifty thousand dollars, were taken from him. Not until seventy years later—thirty years after his death—were Thorpe's medals returned to his heirs. No matter. Medals can come and go, but Jim Thorpe's legend will live forever.

OPPOSITE: **Jim Thorpe was the premier runner of the early days of pro football, but he was even more famed for his spectacular show in the 1912 Olympics.**

LEFT: **Thorpe is shown competing in the shot put in the 1912 Olympics, one of six events he won to capture gold medals in the decathlon and pentathlon. He was stripped of those medals until January 18, 1983, when the International Olympic Committee apologized and returned the medals to his kin.**

STEVE VAN BUREN

When Bucko Kilroy entered the NFL, Nixon was in the navy, FDR was in the White House, and Clinton wasn't even in the womb. Hitler, Mussolini, and Hirohito led the Axis, and Churchill, FDR, and Stalin the Allies. Nobody knew where Korea or Vietnam were. VCRs, personal computers, microwaves, fax machines, and cellular phones didn't exist. Television was some newfangled experiment, and nobody was sure if it would catch on.

The first team Kilroy played for was called the 1943 Phil-Pitt Steagles, a one-year merger of the Philadelphia Eagles and the Pittsburgh Steelers that came about because so many of the teams' players were off to war.

For everything that has happened in the NFL since, Kilroy was there.

All-Pro offensive guard. All-Pro middle guard. Player-coach. Coach. Personnel director. General manager. Vice president. Kilroy's done it all. But mostly, he has earned his paychecks by evaluating talent. He must be pretty good at it, because sixteen general managers and personnel directors got their start with him, and the Patriots still pay for his advice. And so when the NFL put together a blue-ribbon panel to pick its all-time All-Pro team in honor of its seventy-fifth anniversary, it made sure to call Bucko.

When the experts asked his advice about the greatest running backs in NFL history, Bucko named Jim Brown, and all of them nodded their heads. And then he named another guy, and the youngsters blinked and asked, "Who?"

"Steve Van Buren," Kilroy said. "I'm prejudiced; I played with him. But scouting has been my business since I stopped playing and coaching, and not only I but other people use Van Buren as the criterion for what you want in a running back.

"He was the offensive back of the forties, the first real prototype of the modern age. The second prototype would be Jim Brown. They're both, 'How great is

great?' He ran a 9.6 one hundred at 215 pounds. We had a guy named Smackover Scott who ran in the Olympics. He held the U.S. record in the hundred. But over 50 yards, Van Buren was faster.

"Van Buren had a combination of power and speed. He could lower his shoulder and run right through a defensive back. The big thing both Van Buren and Brown had was that they were very instinctive runners. You're talking about the two prototypes that everybody's been looking for ever since."

Not bad accolades for a 125-pound weakling cut by his high school team. Van Buren built his size and strength for two years in an iron foundry, won a scholarship to Louisiana State, and, after serving as the blocking back to future baseball player and manager Alvin Dark, became the star halfback in the Tigers' single wing. The Eagles made him their first-round pick in 1944, and the six-foot-one-inch slasher ran for 129 yards versus the Brooklyn Dodgers and led the league in punt returns as a rookie. The next year, he led the league in rushing, scoring, and kick returns. Two years after that, he became the second NFL player to run for 1,000 yards. Then he did it again in 1949, when he ran for 1,146 yards, a record surpassed only by Brown until the NFL added 2 games to the schedule.

Van Buren led the league in rushing four times, three years consecutively. Only Brown was able to better this feat with eight rushing titles, five consecutively.

Nearly fifty years later, no Eagle has scored more touchdowns in a season or more rushing touchdowns in a season or career. No Eagle has run for more yards in a single game.

Van Buren led the Eagles to their first title game in 1947 and their first championship in 1948, a game he almost didn't make. When he awoke and saw a raging blizzard, he went back to sleep, figuring the game would be postponed. A phone call from coach Greasy Neale woke him up, and he took the trolley toward

Shibe Park, trudging the final seven blocks through the snow. Snow covered the grass, and neither team could move the ball very far. But late in the third quarter, Kilroy recovered a fumble at the Cardinals' 17, and 4 plays later, Van Buren scored the game's only points, single-handedly outrushing the Cardinals' so-called Dream Backfield.

The Eagles repeated as champions when Van Buren ran for 196 yards in the L.A. Coliseum mud, which is still an NFL/NFC championship game record.

"Steve played both ways. He returned punts and kickoffs," Kilroy said. "And he was something Brown was not: he could block with anybody."

He was so ferocious that when his linemen complained that they couldn't handle an opponent, Van Buren demanded the ball and told his teammates to get out of the way. Allie Sherman, then an Eagles assistant, said that Van Buren left the brute laid out—"the only time I ever saw someone's eyes rolling around in his head like in a Laurel and Hardy movie."

Steve Van Buren (15) trudges past two Chicago Cardinals through five inches of snow as he leads the Philadelphia Eagles to the 1948 NFL title. Van Buren ran for the game's only score after Bucko Kilroy (76) picked up a Chicago fumble.

HALL OF FAME RUNNING BACKS

Of the 180 players in the Hall of Fame, backs are well represented (36):

CLIFF BATTLES: Boston Braves (1932), Boston Redskins (1933–1936), Washington Redskins (1937)

JIM BROWN: Cleveland Browns (1957–1965)

EARL CAMPBELL: Houston Oilers (1978–1984), New Orleans Saints (1984–1985)

TONY CANADEO: Green Bay Packers (1941–1944, 1946–1952)

LARRY CSONKA: Miami Dolphins (1968–1974, 1979), New York Giants (1976–1978), Memphis Southmen (WFL, 1975)

TONY DORSETT: Dallas Cowboys (1977–1987), Denver Broncos (1988)

"BULLET" BILL DUDLEY: Pittsburgh Steelers (1942, 1945–1946), Detroit Lions (1947–1949), Washington Redskins (1950–1951, 1953)

FRANK GIFFORD: New York Giants (1952–1960, 1962–1964)

RED GRANGE: Chicago Bears (1925, 1929–1934), New York Yankees (1926–1927)

JOE GUYON: Canton Bulldogs (1920), Cleveland Indians (1921), Oorang Indians (1922–1923), Rock Island Independents (1924), Kansas City Cowboys (1924–1925), New York Giants (1927)

FRANCO HARRIS: Pittsburgh Steelers (1972–1983), Seattle Seahawks (1984)

CLARKE HINKLE: Green Bay Packers (1932–1941)

PAUL HORNUNG: Green Bay Packers (1957–1962, 1964–1966)

JOHN HENRY JOHNSON: San Francisco 49ers (1954–1956), Detroit Lions (1957–1959), Pittsburgh Steelers (1960–1965), Houston Oilers (1966)

LEROY KELLY: Cleveland Browns (1964–1973)

TUFFY LEEMANS: New York Giants (1936–1943)

OLLIE MATSON: Chicago Cardinals (1952, 1954–1958), Los Angeles Rams (1959–1962), Detroit Lions (1963), Philadelphia Eagles (1964–1966)

GEORGE MCAFEE: Chicago Bears (1940–1941, 1945–1950)

HUGH MCELHENNY: San Francisco 49ers (1952–1960), Minnesota Vikings (1961–1962), New York Giants (1963), Detroit Lions (1964)

JOHNNY "BLOOD" MCNALLY: Milwaukee Badgers (1925–1926), Duluth Eskimos (1926–1927), Pottsville Maroons (1928), Green Bay Packers (1929–1933, 1935–1936), Pittsburgh Pirates (1934, 1937–1939 as player-coach)

BOBBY MITCHELL: Cleveland Browns (1958–1961), Washington Redskins (1962–1968)

LENNY MOORE: Baltimore Colts (1956–1967)

MARION MOTLEY: Cleveland Browns (1946–1953), Pittsburgh Steelers (1955)

BRONKO NAGURSKI: Chicago Bears (1930–1937, 1943)

ERNIE NEVERS: Duluth Eskimos (1926–1927), Chicago Cardinals (1929–1931)

WALTER PAYTON: Chicago Bears (1975–1987)

JOE PERRY: San Francisco 49ers (1948–1960, 1963), Baltimore Colts (1961–1962)

JOHN RIGGINS: New York Jets (1971–1975), Washington Redskins (1976–1979, 1981–1985)

GALE SAYERS: Chicago Bears (1965–1971)

O.J. SIMPSON: Buffalo Bills (1969–1977), San Francisco 49ers (1978–1979)

KEN STRONG: Staten Island Stapletons (1929–1932), New York Giants (1933–1935, 1939, 1944–1947), New York Yanks (1936–1937)

JIM TAYLOR: Green Bay Packers (1958–1966), New Orleans Saints (1967)

JIM THORPE: Canton Bulldogs (1915–1917, 1919–1920, 1926), Cleveland Indians (1921), Oorang Indians (1922–1923), Rock Island Independents (1924), New York Giants (1925), Chicago Cardinals (1928)

CHARLEY TRIPPI: Chicago Cardinals (1947–1955)

STEVE VAN BUREN: Philadelphia Eagles (1944–1951)

DOAK WALKER: Detroit Lions (1950–1955)

TOP ALL-TIME RUSHERS

Player	Years	Attempts	Yards	Average	TDs
1. Walter Payton	13	3,838	16,726	4.4	110
2. Eric Dickerson	11	2,996	13,259	4.4	90
3. Tony Dorsett	12	2,936	12,739	4.3	77
4. Jim Brown	9	2,359	12,312	5.2	106
5. Franco Harris	13	2,949	12,120	4.1	91
6. John Riggins	14	2,916	11,352	3.9	104
7. O.J. Simpson	11	2,404	11,236	4.7	61
8. Marcus Allen	14*	2,692	10,908	4.1	103
9. Ottis Anderson	14	2,562	10,273	4.0	81
10. Barry Sanders	7*	2,077	10,172	4.9	73
11. Thurman Thomas	8*	2,285	9,729	4.3	54
12. Earl Campbell	8	2,187	9,407	4.3	74
13. Emmitt Smith	6*	2,007	8,956	4.5	96
14. Jim Taylor	10	1,941	8,597	4.4	83
15. Joe Perry	14	1,737	8,378	4.8	58
16. Roger Craig	11	1,991	8,189	4.1	56
17. Gerald Riggs	10	1,989	8,188	4.1	69
18. Herschel Walker	10*	1,938	8,122	4.2	60
19. Larry Csonka	11	1,891	8,081	4.3	64
20. Freeman McNeil	12	1,798	8,074	4.5	38

* indicates active

BIBLIOGRAPHY

King, Peter. *Football: A History of the Professional Game*. New York: Time-Life Books, 1993.

McDonough, Will, ed. *75 Seasons: The Complete Story of the National Football League, 1920–1995*. Atlanta, Ga.: Turner Publishing, 1994.

National Football League Staff, ed. *The Official National Football League 1995 Record & Fact Book*. New York: NFL, 1995.

Smith, Don. *Pro Football Hall of Fame All-Time Greats*. New York: Gallery Books, 1988.

PHOTOGRAPHY CREDITS

INDEX